TOP WALKS IN WEST CORNWALL

LIZ HURLEY

MUDLARK'S PRESS

Top Walks in West Cornwall

Copyright © 2023 Liz Hurley.

First Edition, 2023

ISBN: 978-1-913628-11-6

Maps created on InkAtlas.com. Copyright OpenStreetMap contributors.

Walk locations map by Google.

Photography by Liz Hurley.

A CIP catalogue record for this book is available from the British Library.

Mudlark's Press

www.lizhurleywrites.com

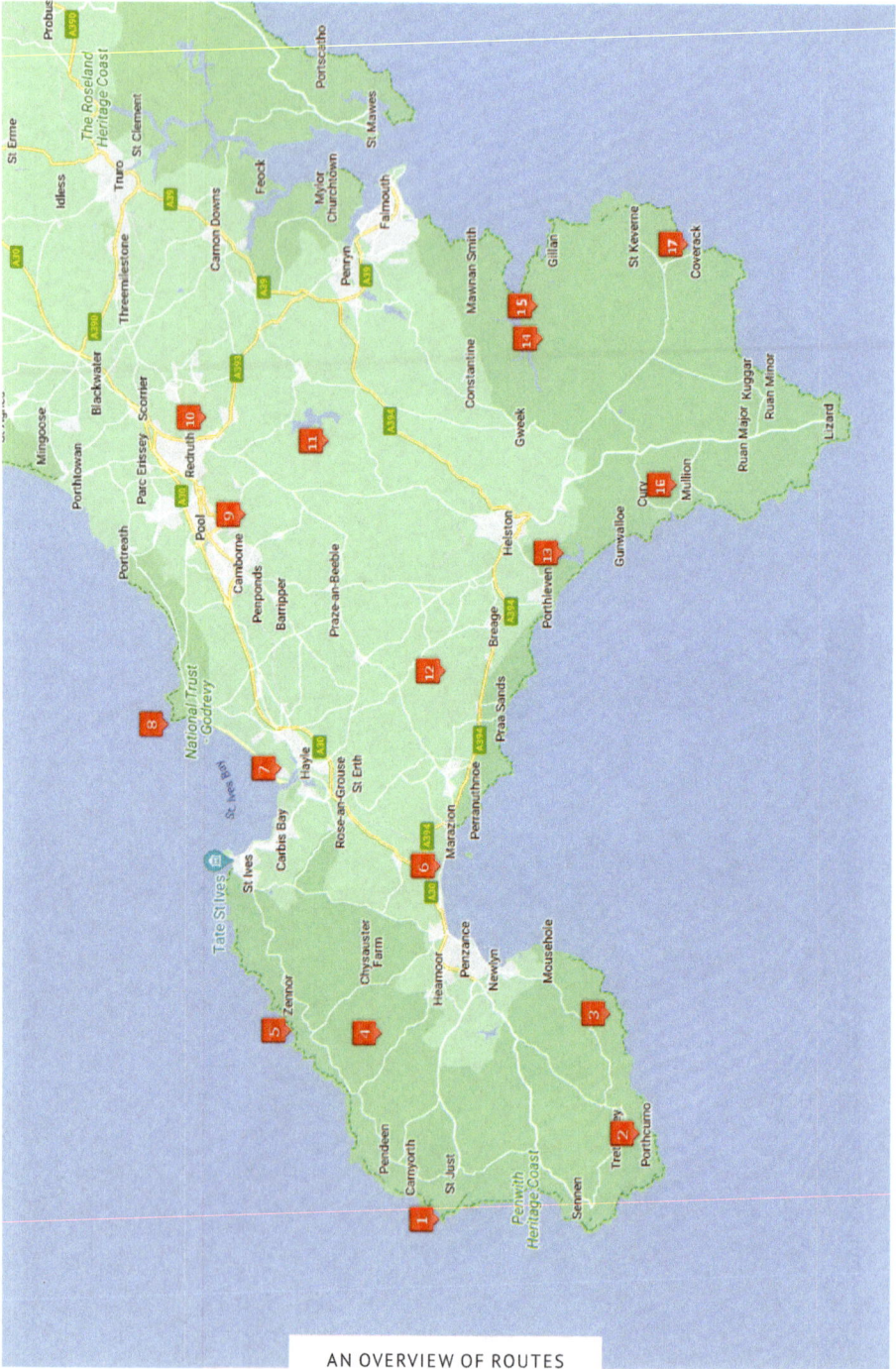

AN OVERVIEW OF ROUTES

CONTENTS

INTRODUCTION

Welcome to *Top Walks in West Cornwall*. This series is designed to show you the very best parts of Cornwall and features a wide range of walks.

These walks have been extensively tested and are widely praised for their ease of use and accuracy. However, we always recommend you carry an Ordnance Survey (OS) map with you, and a GPS app on your phone is also a useful tool.

Nearly all the walks are circular so you can walk in either direction, although the guide only explains the route one way. If you want a longer walk, just turn around and retrace your footsteps for a change of scenery. Some of the shorter walks have a neighbouring walk that they can be linked to.

If you do all the walks and their extensions in this book, you will have walked over 85 miles. You will have walked past iconic lighthouses and World Heritage mining complexes. You will have retraced the footsteps of Phoenician traders and ancient saints, following streams and rivers down to the sea and beyond. You will have stood in the place of romantic creeks and hidden wonders and hopefully also spotted some Cornish wildlife as well.

As these are largely countryside or coastal walks, the majority are not suitable for wheelchairs or buggies.

Each walk is accompanied by notes about various sights along the route. These interesting snippets help bring the walk to life. The guide also recommends other nearby attractions as well as great places to eat and drink locally.

Added extras

In this day and age, a book can only be enhanced by adding in links to further information. Each walk features links, as well as a .gpx file of the walk.

https://cornishwalks.com/gpx-files-top-walks-in-west-cornwall/

In the print book, I have shortened long web addresses for ease of typing but have left easily typed links as they are. In the e-book all hyperlinks are active.

TIPS AND ADVICE

Countryside Code

- Respect the people who live and work in the countryside. Respect private property, farmland and all rural environments.

- Do not interfere with livestock, machinery and crops.

- Respect and, where possible, protect all wildlife, plants and trees.

- When walking, use the approved routes and keep as closely as possible to them.

- Take special care when walking on country roads.

- Leave all gates as you find them and do not interfere with or damage any gates, fences, walls or hedges.

- Guard against all risks of fire, especially near forests.

- Always keep children closely supervised while on a walk.

- Do not walk the Ways in large groups and always maintain a low profile.

- Take all litter home, leaving only footprints behind.

- Keep the number of cars used to the minimum and park carefully to avoid blocking farm gateways or narrow roads.

- Minimise impact on fragile vegetation and soft ground.

- Take heed of warning signs – they are there for your protection.

Cattle

If you find yourself in a field of suddenly wary cattle, move away as carefully and quietly as possible. If you feel threatened by cattle then let go of your dog's lead and let it run free rather than try to protect it and endanger yourself. The dog will outrun the cows, and it will also outrun you.

Those without canine companions should follow similar advice: move away calmly, do not panic and make no sudden noises. Chances are the cows will leave you alone once they establish that you pose no threat.

If you walk through a field of cows and there happen to be calves, be vigilant as mothers can be more protective. If crossing a field with cattle in, you don't need to stick to the footpath if you wish to avoid them. By all means skirt around the edge of the field.

Remain quiet. Cows are curious and if they hear a lot of noise they will come over and investigate.

Walking With Dogs

The coast path is unfenced, and the cliffs can have sheer drops. Every year dogs die running off the edge, so it is always safest to keep your dog on a lead.

Please pick up after your dogs and always take the bag home if you can't find a bin.

All the walks in this book are suitable for dogs on leads.

Adder Bites

While uncommon, adder bites are something to be aware of during summer. A bite can be unpleasant but the last fatality was 1975, so it certainly shouldn't cause you to avoid a walk. If a dog or a small child gets bitten get them to medical attention immediately without causing any stress or panic. Carry them rather than make them walk.

GUIDE TO THE LEGEND

Before heading off for a walk read the description first as you may discover issues with it, such as cows, tides, number of stiles or mud. Then have a look at a map – not just the little one provided with the walk – to get a proper feel for the direction of the walk.

Additional Information: Some walks may be hampered by the tide or weather, or may be improved by a few specific suggestions. Detail will be given here.

Optional Walk: Occasionally, a walk will have a smaller side walk nearby. This won't be described in length but mentioned as a suggestion.

Length: This has been calculated using a range of GPS tracking devices, but ultimately we have used the Ordnance Survey route tracker. This will generally differ from a pedometer.

Effort: 'Easy' to 'Challenging'. These descriptions are only in relation to each other in this book. Every walk has at least one hill in it; not everyone finds hills easy. 'Challenging' is for the hardest walks in the book and is based on effort and duration. However, nothing in here is particularly tortuous.

Terrain: If it's been raining a lot, please assume that footpaths will be muddy. Coastal paths tend to be a bit better, but near villages they tend to be a bit worse. Towards the end of summer vegetation may obscure the path and signposts.

Livestock: It is possible that you won't encounter any livestock on a walk that mentions them. Please read the Countryside Code section on how to avoid them if you do.

Parking: The postcode for satnav is given, but when a specific car park is mentioned be aware that Cornwall is not always kind to satnavs. Have a road map to hand and check you know where you are heading before you set off.

Toilets: Due to Council cuts, lots of loos are now closed or run by local parishes with seasonal opening hours. If they are an essential part of your walk, check online first. Lots are now coin operated.

Café / Pub: These are local recommendations. Always check ahead as some will have seasonal opening hours.

OS Map: This will be the largest scale available for the area.

Nearby Attractions: These are sites worth visiting within a short drive of the walk's location. Some will be seasonal and may have an admission charge.

Directions: If I say, 'going up the road', *up* or *down* means there is a slope. If I refer to north or SW you will need a compass. Most smartphones have built-in compasses, but it isn't essential as other directions will be given. However, it will be a useful aid, especially in woodland where there are few other clues.

FINALLY

Things change: trees fall down, posts get broken, signs become obscured and footpaths can be closed for repair. Don't be alarmed if you can't see a marker. Follow the rest of the instructions and only retrace your steps if you are convinced you are off route. A walking app is invaluable when used with the .gpx files provided free with this book.

1

CAPE CORNWALL TO BOTALLACK – 5 MILES

Cracking views, rolling landscapes, historic landmarks, industrial archaeology and a sea pool. This really is a walk for everyone. Get your camera ready, there's so much to see. To make the walk shorter there are two sections that can be lopped off, making this a 3.5 mile walk.

Length: 5 miles
Effort: Moderate
Terrain: Coast path, paved tracks, fields
Livestock: Some potential for sheep
Parking: National Trust Cape Cornwall Car Park, TR19 7NN
Toilets: Botallack National Trust Café
Café / Pub: Botallack National Trust Café
OS Map: 102

Nearby Attractions:
- Cape Cornwall sea pool
- Geevor Tin Mine Museum

🌐 https://cornishwalks.com/gpx-files-top-walks-in-west-cornwall/

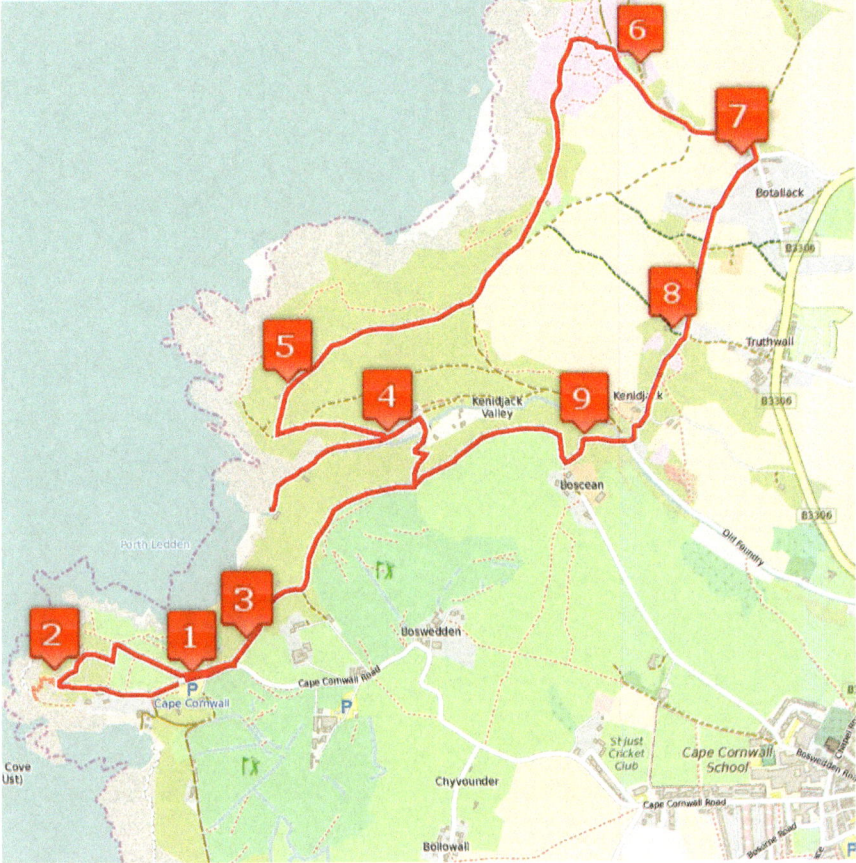

Elevation Profile

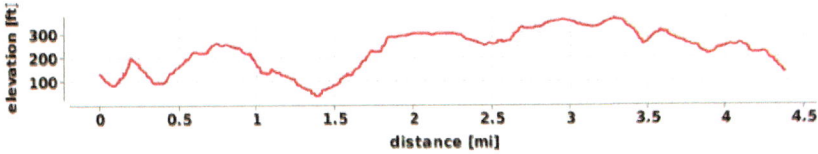

DIRECTIONS:

If you want, you can start this walk at Step 3, leaving off Cape Cornwall. From the car park cross the road and take the footpath heading uphill. This will remove half a mile.

1. From the National Trust car park, head onto the road and walk downhill. You will be walking up to the large chimney on the hill ahead of you. At the road gate, pass through on the

left, heading towards some private dwellings. Take the path to the right-hand side of a house and start to climb. The path splits on the way up to the summit. One path is easier than the other but both arrive at the same point.

2. Having enjoyed the view from **Cape Cornwall** head downhill. With your back to the sea and the chimney behind you take the left-hand path heading downhill. At the bottom of the hill turn left at the stone wall and start heading downhill towards the sea. At the next junction turn right and follow the coast path signs. The path cuts across a large field, passing a circular cross and **St Helen's Oratory**. The path heads uphill and then runs alongside the road. Stay on this side of the wall and as the path reaches an unmade lane, turn left onto it.

3. Stay on this path for half a mile until you reach the small bridge at the bottom of the valley. There are a couple of junctions but at each point there is a coast path marker and you should take the signs towards Botallack. Be aware that these are small markers and may be obscured by plants. Cross over the small stone bridge and then turn left at the next junction heading downhill. Shortly afterwards the path splits with the right-hand path heading uphill and continuing the route to Botallack. We shall continue on this path later, but for now, head downhill into the beautiful **Kenidjack Valley**. This extension is one mile there and back and can be skipped if desired.

4. Having explored this hidden valley down to the sea and past a range of industrial buildings, head back up to the coast path junction and walk uphill. When you reach a T-junction turn left and follow the coast path to

i **Cape Cornwall**
The mine is situated on the westernmost point of Cornwall and was primarily a tin mining operation. It ran on and off from 1838 until its final closure in 1883, when its engine house was also taken down. However, the chimney built in 1864 near the cape's summit was preserved as a navigational aid.

The tidal pool in Priest Cove was built in the 1950s for local children to swim safely.

i **St Helen's Oratory**
This small early-Christian chapel is believed by some to trace back to the Roman era. A historic cross featuring a chi-rho symbol was unearthed at the location in the 1800s but unfortunately went missing. The cross currently adorning the chapel was discovered in the vicinity.

i **Kenidjack Valley**
Kenidjack Valley serves as a captivating intersection of natural splendour and historical significance. Once vital

for its tin and copper mines, some of which are believed to date back to ancient times, the valley now draws visitors with its scenic beauty. Features like craggy cliffs, lush hills and sweeping views of the Atlantic Ocean make the landscape irresistibly picturesque, and the region is home to diverse plant and animal life. The presence of ancient field systems and remnants of old mining structures adds a historical layer to the valley, appealing to both nature aficionados and history buffs.

Botallack. After a short climb you will see a ruined building ahead of you, this is the remains of a store house built for a rifle range. It sits on the same site as Kenidjack Castle.

5.   From the castle take any path to rejoin the coast path keeping the sea on your left. Ahead you will begin to see a collection of ruined industrial structures. At one point the path splits with the Public Byway pointing towards Botallack. Ignore this and instead take the lower left-hand coast path towards Levant. This path will take you through the **Botallack Mines** complex.

This is a sprawling area of fascinating buildings so take time to explore all

there is. Then make your way to the visitors' centre and tea shop, which is located in Botallack Count House, a fine, large Georgian building.

6. With the Count House behind you, turn left along the unmade road heading away from the sea. After a short while the lane ends at a T-junction in a small hamlet. Turn right, walk a few yards along the tarmac and then turn right again down an unmade lane. Follow this lane and when it bends sharply to the right, walk forwards onto a footpath. The path runs along the left-hand side of Parknoweth Cottage and its garden.

Botallack Mines

Botallack Mines are part of the Cornwall and West Devon Mining Landscape, a UNESCO World Heritage site. The mines are perhaps most famous for the Crowns Engine Houses, which are dramatically situated on cliffs overlooking the Atlantic Ocean. Operating from the eighteenth to the late nineteenth century, these mines were a significant part of Cornwall's tin and copper mining industry. Fans of Poldark will recognise many of the views.

7.   Take the footpath across the field and exit via the gate or stile and walk towards a large track. Follow the track in the direction of the house on the skyline. At the T-junction with another track, turn right, walking in front of the house. Take the left-hand track directly in front of the house. Ahead you can see a mining chimney in the distance.

8.   Stay on this path, walking straight ahead, crossing a series of granite stiles until you come down into some farm buildings. Continue downhill. When you reach a small road cross over and then cross the

small stream. Take the wide track uphill with a large chimney up to your left.

9. Climb up the path until just before you arrive at a little collection of cottages. Turn right, following the sign to Cape Cornwall. Take this path all the way back to the beginning of the walk. Along the way you will rejoin your original path and simply follow the signs to Cape Cornwall. From the car park it's a short walk down to Priest Cove, a pretty little beach with a sea pool.

LINKS:

Botallack
https://www.nationaltrust.org.uk/visit/cornwall/botallack

Cape Cornwall
https://www.nationaltrust.org.uk/visit/cornwall/cape-cornwall

2

PORTHCURNO – 4 MILES

A short walk that will give you a good work out. As a reward you will pass some of Cornwall's most beautiful beaches, pause for a swim and explore The Minack, an open-air theatre carved into the rock. Return via fields and explore where the first undersea telegraph cables were laid in 1870.

Length: 4 miles
Effort: Moderate
Terrain: Coast path, paved tracks, fields
Livestock: Some potential for sheep
Parking: Treen Car Park, TR19 6LF
Toilets: Treen, Porthcurno
Café / Pub: The Logan Rock Inn, Treen
OS Map: 102

Nearby Attractions:
- PK Porthcurno Museum of Global Communications
- The Minack Theatre

🌐 https://cornishwalks.com/gpx-files-top-walks-in-west-cornwall/

Elevation Profile

DIRECTIONS:

1. Leave the car park, heading back to the houses and turn left at the public loos, heading along the tarmac. There is a hard-to-spot left-hand turning off the lane running alongside Logan Cottage. It is signposted to Logan's Rock. This is your footpath. Head along the footpath, over a flight of granite steps and onto a wide footpath. After about 20 metres, the footpath veers off to the right cutting across a field. You are walking in

White Pyramid
The pyramid stands at the point where a hut that housed the termination of a submarine telegraph cable connected to the French port of Brest once stood. Fishermen began to use the hut as a point of reference, so when it was

the direction of the sea and following directions to Logan's Rock.

2. Follow the path down through the fields until you come onto the coast path, now turn right and follow the coast path to Porthcurno. There are options along the way to either take the bridle path or the coastal path. Both travel in the same direction so the choice is yours. The coast path obviously goes closer to the sea, but is more rugged. Having passed above the Pedn Vounder Beach and the White Pyramid, after a while the path splits again, with the left-hand path heading in the direction of a large metal, diamond shaped sign. This path takes

pulled down it was replaced with the pyramid. The pyramid is three metres tall and painted white. No fisherman is going to miss that.

Pedn Vounder Beach
A glorious beach, but access is difficult and you'll need both hands free to climb up and down the rocks. No lifeguard cover and some strong riptides.

you down onto the beach and is a rocky descent. If you want an easier route stay on the bridle path and when you reach the road turn left and head down to the coastguard station.

3. Having had fun on the Porthcurno beach, head back onto the coast path. There is a flight of stone steps leading directly off the beach on the right. Alternatively head back to the coastguard station and take the coast path uphill. This becomes very steep as you head up and there is a banister by the steps which will be greatly appreciated. At the top walk alongside The Minack Theatre and into the first car park. The coast path continues from the top right of this car park.

4. Continue along the footpath until you cross a wooden bridge and reach St Levan's Holy Well. This is where you leave the coast path. Take the footpath on your right. This path is nice and shady. At the junction with another footpath turn right, walking towards the houses. As you come onto a lane, head towards the church and into the graveyard. The exit is in the top-left of the graveyard via an impressive lychgate. There is also a huge split boulder in the graveyard. It is said this was split by St Levan, and if the gap ever becomes wide enough for a horse with panniers to pass through, the world will end.

Porthcurno

Porthcurno holds historical significance as a major international hub for submarine telegraph cables. In the nineteenth and twentieth centuries, it served as the landing point for numerous telegraph cables that connected Britain to various parts of the world, including the British Empire. The village was essentially the nexus of a global communication network long before the advent of the internet, playing a vital role in international communications.

St Levan's Holy Well

This well is renowned for its supposed healing powers, attracting pilgrims and visitors seeking physical or spiritual relief. In keeping with an ancient Celtic custom that blends with Christian practices, the area around the well is often adorned with *clouties*, or small strips of cloth.

Minack Theatre

The Minack Theatre is an open-air theatre created by Rowena Cade, who lived in Minack House adjacent to the site. The theatre started as a simple stage for a local production of *A Midsummer Night's Dream* in 1932 and evolved into the grand structure it is today. Built primarily of concrete mixed with local beach sand, the theatre offers a stunning backdrop of the Atlantic Ocean, making it one of the most visually impressive performing arts venues in the world.

19

5.   Walk uphill, crossing two fields. In the second field the exit is in front of the houses. Turn left in front of the houses and take the unmade road down to the main road. Head straight across the road and take the footpath uphill as it winds behind the back of the PK Porthcurno Museum. Just as you reach the gate entrance to the museum, the footpath heads off on the left-hand side up a steep, grassy slope.

6.   The path crosses scrubland and into a field. Cut straight across the next field in the direction of the houses. In the next field head towards a telegraph pole to the right of the houses. Head along the farm lane and as you pass the farmhouse take the footpath on your right into the field. Keep to the left of the field and exit via the top-left corner. The path now continues in a straight line across a series of fields. The route is clear as you head back to the start of your walk. Finally, you pass a cottage and head down into Treen. Turn right and return to the car park.

LINKS:

PK Porthcurno Museum of Global Communications
https://pkporthcurno.com/

The Minack Theatre
https://minack.com/

3

LAMORNA TO ST LOY – 5 MILES

The first half of this walk is challenging with spectacular views. The second half explores a variety of ancient monuments. From coast paths, wooded valleys and babbling streams on to fields and ancient monuments, this is a taxing but fabulous walk.

Length: 5 miles
Effort: Challenging. Stout footwear is strongly recommended
Terrain: Coast path, paved tracks, fields
Livestock: Some potential for sheep and cattle. Alternate route suggested
Parking: Lamorna Cove Car Park, TR19 6XQ. This can get busy and there is limited alternative parking. They are also ticket-happy so don't underpay or park on the lines!
Toilets: Lamorna Cove
Café / Pub: Lamorna Wink pub, Lamorna Cove Café
OS Map: 102

Nearby Attractions:
- Mousehole
- Carn Euny
- The Minack Theatre

https://cornishwalks.com/gpx-files-top-walks-in-west-cornwall/

Elevation Profile

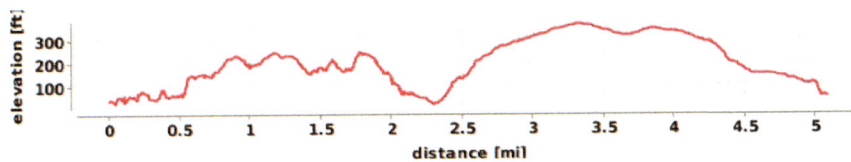

DIRECTIONS:

1. Start the walk from Lamorna Cove car park. Head out onto the coast path and turn right, the sea should be on your left. Follow the coast path for about two and a half miles until you reach St Loy's Cove. Just after the first mile you will pass the Tater-du Lighthouse. This whole section of the coast path can be quite strenuous. Several sections are also along a stream that gets very boggy. You also pass through the landscape made famous by **Derek Tangye and the 'Minack Chronicles'**.

Derek Tangye and the 'Minack Chronicles'

Derek Tangye was a British author famous for his 'Minack Chronicles', a series of autobiographical books detailing his and his wife Jeannie's decision to abandon urban life in London for a simpler existence in Cornwall. Set around their cottage, the series explores their

2.   Eventually the coast path comes down onto St Loy's Cove, which is covered in small boulders. Walk along the beach, keeping to the top. After about 25 metres keep an eye out for a turning off the beach.

3.   Follow the path as it crosses a small stream and start heading uphill. Cross a private drive and continue uphill following the coast path signs. The path now goes up a flight of irregular steps, it's quite a workout. At the top there is a right-hand turn, heading inland. Climb over the stile and take this footpath walking uphill and away from the coast path.

4.   Follow the footpath over the stepping-stones, across the stream, and then turn left. Head uphill along the stream. You are looking for a turning off this footpath to the right. It's not obvious.

interactions with local wildlife, their efforts at self-sufficiency, and their deep connection to the Cornish landscape.

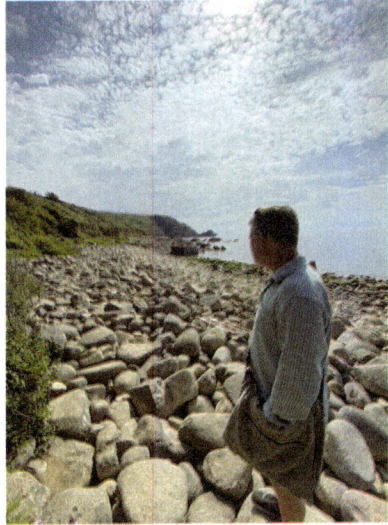

There's absolutely no markings to suggest it's there, but if you're looking out for it, you will see it. There is a big boulder to the left of the path and just after that there is a small path to the right, climbing up through the roots of a large tree and you will come onto a private drive. Turn left and now head uphill.

5.   Stay on this drive all the way up through a small hamlet called Boskenna. After the hamlet as the drive bends sharply to the left, the footpath continues straight ahead through the metal gate. Cross the field on a left-hand diagonal towards the telegraph poles. At the far end exit via the top left-hand corner via a granite stile and into a lay-by.

Note. Sometimes there are cattle in this field. If you wish to avoid the cattle stay on the drive until it reaches the main road and turn right until you get to the Boskenna Cross, which is where the footpath through the field rejoins the road.

6. Leave the field. **Boskenna Cross** is just to your left. The rest of the walk is now flat or downhill. Turn right and walk along the road. This road is a main road, and although it is generally quiet and wide, care will still need to be taken. After a third of a mile, you pass **Tregiffian Burial Chamber** on your right. Shortly after that is another lay-by with a bus stop by it. Take the stile into the field, where you can see the **Merry Maidens Stone Circle**.

7. Walk directly through the circle and continue on the path. Exit the field via the

Boskenna Stone Cross
The Boskenna Stone Cross has endured a turbulent history. Originally discovered in a hedgerow in 1869, it was likely hidden there during the Reformation, a practice common in Cornwall. While only the top part of the cross is original, it was later mounted on a combination of granite shafts and plinths. The back of the cross shows the Christ figure. Despite being relocated near a road for visibility, it was struck by a lorry. The cross was then moved to its current location but has been struck a further two times.

Tregiffian Burial Chamber
This ancient megalithic tomb dates back to the late neolithic or early Bronze Age. It features a unique 'entrance grave' design, consisting of a stone-lined chamber covered by a large capstone and partially set into a mound. Adding to the site's intrigue

granite stiles in the top left-hand corner. In the next field cut diagonally across the field in the direction of the telegraph pole in the middle of the field. Exit the field just before the next telegraph pole, and climb down to the road.

8.   Turn right. You are at the junction of three roads. You need to pick the middle one heading towards a dead end, not the main road to the left or the right-hand drive. Stay on the road as it peters out. Head downhill into the trees and then take the bridleway down into Lamorna Valley. When the track joins the road, turn right and follow it all the way down to the village and your car park.

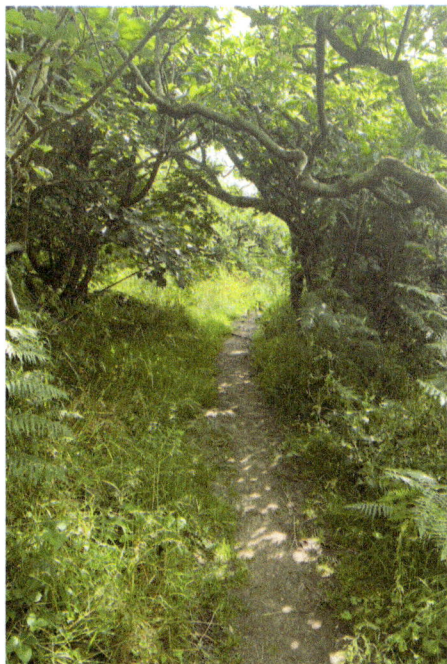

are mysterious 'cup marks': round depressions carved into the stone. Their purpose remains unclear but they may have ritualistic or symbolic significance.

Merry Maidens Stone Circle

According to local folklore, the circle was formed when 19 maidens were turned to stone as punishment for dancing on a Sunday. Two nearby standing stones, known as the Pipers, are said to be the petrified remains of the musicians who played for the dancers.

LINKS:

Ancient sites in Cornwall
https://cornishancientsites.com/ancient-sites/

4
....

WEST PENWITH MOOR – 6 MILES

An invigorating walk across some of Cornwall's oldest inhabited landscape. This landscape is wild and remote and pretty wonderful. The walk passes a rich concentration of ancient monuments, including Mên-an-Tol, standing stones, stone circles and quoits, as well as the natural features of carns and streams and the more recent structures of Ding Dong Mine and Carn Galver Mine.

Additional Information

Signposting: Much of this walk is on open moorland. There are almost no signposts, and while the footpaths are mostly obvious you need to have a good line of sight to follow the directions. Best done in good visibility. In high summer the vegetation will also make some of the paths tricky.

Length: 6 miles
Effort: Moderate
Terrain: Moorland paths and tracks
Livestock: Some potential for sheep, cattle and horses
Parking: Carn Galver National Trust Car Park, TR20 8YX
Toilets: None on walk. Closest facilities at the Gurnard's Head for patrons
Café / Pub: The Gurnard's Head
OS Map: 102

Nearby Attractions:
- Chysauster Settlement
- Botallack Mines
- Zennor

🌐 https://cornishwalks.com/gpx-files-top-walks-in-west-cornwall/

Elevation Profile

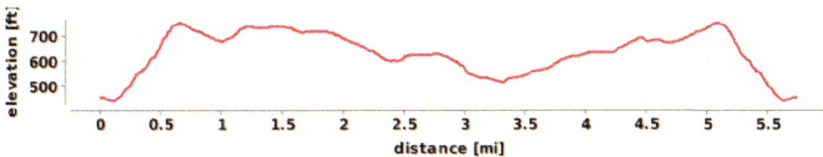

DIRECTIONS:

1. From the National Trust car park at Carn Galver, turn right and walk along the road. Just after the cattle grid, turn left onto the public footpath which heads up onto the moor. The path continues uphill between Carn Galver to your left and Watch Croft, to your right. The path is rocky, uneven and often wet.

2. At the summit the path becomes broader. On the horizon ahead of you is Ding Dong Engine House, a large building

Boundary Stone
This is a large recumbent boundary stone with an incised cross. This stone marks the meeting of the four ancient parishes of Zennor, Morvah, Gulval and Madron.

with an even larger chimney beside it. Continue through the kissing gate and head forward in the direction of the engine house.

3. Continue downhill until the path opens up to a green clearing. Walk forwards until you reach a large flat stone known as the **Boundary Stone** or Four Parishes Stone. From here the path forks, take the left-hand path. After several metres, the path splits again take the right-hand path. Follow the path uphill until it levels out. Stay on this track eventually you will see a group of standing stones ahead. These are the **Nine Maidens**.

4. Walk through the stone circle and then take the path out of the circle, heading in the direction of the chimney stack. As you walk along this path, if you're lucky, over to your left you'll get some beautiful views of Saint Michael's Mount down in the bay.

5. Where the path joins a rough track, turn right and walk in the direction of **Ding Dong Mine**. As you reach the mine take the left-hand path, directly passing the mine on your right. Cross over wooden steps and take the grass path heading downhill.

6. When you get down to the large metal gate, pass through and then take

Nine Maidens

Like many stone circles in Cornwall, these were said to be a group of maidens caught dancing on the Sabbath and turned to stone. It's uncertain what stone circles were used for, but astronomical clocks seem to be the leading theory.

Ding Dong Mine

Located in West Cornwall, it is said to be one of the oldest mines in the county. Mining activity in the Ding Dong area may trace back to prehistoric times, potentially as early as the Bronze Age. The name possibly derives from the sound of the machines down the shaft.

the footpath to your left, heading in the direction of a telegraph pole. Pass **Bosiliack Chambered Cairn** on your left, a round collection of large upright stones: it always reminds me of a crown. As you continue downhill **Lanyon Quoit** is now directly ahead of you, but you may not yet be able to pick it out. As the path drops the quoit will be framed on the skyline and easier to spot. When the path starts to head uphill again there are a few splits. Try to keep to the left-hand fork and then head between two large wooden posts. If you reach a shiny metal gate, turn left and walk down to the wooden posts, pass

Bosiliack Chambered Cairn

This is an entrance grave, which is a specific type of prehistoric burial monument found predominantly in the Isles of Scilly and Cornwall's Penwith peninsula. These entrance graves, like Bosiliack Barrow, were communal burial sites. Over time the remains of several individuals, often in a disarticulated state, would be placed inside.

through them and start walking uphill. At the brow of the hill, the quoit should be ahead of you slightly to your left.

7.   From the quoit, turn right and walk out onto the road via a granite stile. Now turn right and walk along the road.

It is possible to get to **Mên-an-Tol** across the moor, but in winter the path is often flooded and in summer it's often over-grown, so with a lovely quiet tarmac road at our disposal, we may as well take that.

Stay on the road for just under a mile, until you get to a small car park and a sign pointing to Mên-an-Tol. Opposite the turning is an old granite building with the date 1882 on its wall.

Lanyon Quoit
The quoit is believed to date back to the neolithic period, around 4000–2500 BC. Such structures were often communal burial sites and would be covered in earth. The quoit wasn't always in its current form. In 1815 it collapsed during a storm and when it was reconstructed in 1824 it was reportedly shorter than its original height as not all of the original stones were used. This is the structure we see today.

8. Leave the road and take the track on your right. This is the ancient **Tinners Way**. Head uphill for half a mile. There is a clear turning on the right-hand side over a set of granite steps with the sign-post, pointing to Mên-an-Tol. It's about a hundred metres to the stones. Having explored them, return to the Tinners Way.

9. Continue uphill along the track for another two hundred metres. When you reach a metal gate, there is a set of granite steps heading into a field, in the middle of which is an inscribed stone known as **Mên Scryfa**. This is private land, but the farmer allows access to walk towards the stone and examine it. Don't try to exit the field via any other route: come back to these granite steps. Once back on the track continue forward.

10. As the path widens out you pass a very derelict stone cottage, and then you'll come to a collection of footpaths in a crossroads. You should now recognise that you are back at the boundary stone. Turn left, walking towards Carn Galver, and retrace your steps back to your car.

Mên-an-Tol

Mên-an-Tol is steeped in local folklore. One of the most enduring beliefs is that it has healing properties, particularly for back problems or rickets. People would pass through the hole in the stone – often three times – in a bid to cure ailments. Children were often passed through the hole as a rite of passage or to cure them of various diseases.

Tinners Way

The path's roots date back to the Bronze Age and possibly even earlier. It has been used by various peoples over millennia, from ancient settlers to medieval tin miners. The Tinners Way runs across the Penwith Peninsula, traversing from St Just in the west to St Ives in the north. Along its course, it passes through a landscape rich in archaeological sites, including stone circles, standing stones and ancient settlements.

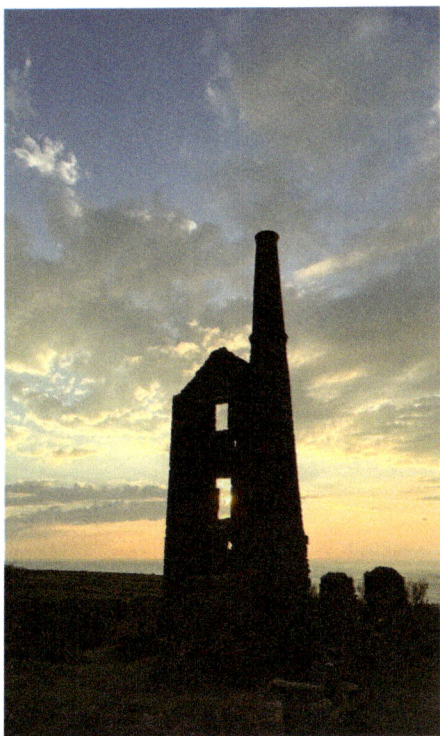

Mên Scryfa

The stone is inscribed with the Latin characters RIALOBRANI CUNOVALI FILI, which in Cornish means 'Royal Raven Son of the Glorious Prince'. Likely dating to the fifth or sixth century AD, the stone stands as a testament to Cornwall's early post-Roman history.

LINKS:

West Penwith
https://www.cornwall-aonb.gov.uk/westpenwith

5

GURNARD'S HEAD – 5.5 MILES

A glorious walk of two halves. The first section along the coast path looks down on amazing beaches as the path clambers up and down valleys and over rocks. The path then heads inland along small lanes and fields, surrounded by the stunning Penwith landscape.

Length: 5.5 miles

Effort: Challenging first half. Easy second half. Stout footwear is strongly recommended

Terrain: Uneven, rocky coast path, fields, lanes

Livestock: Some potential for sheep and cattle. You can walk along the road if preferred

Parking: Zennor Car Park, TR26 3DA

Toilets: There are no public loos but there are two pubs and a café along the way

Café / Pub: The Tinners Arms, Zennor; Moomaid Café, Zennor; The Gurnard's Head, Treen

OS Map: Explorer 102

Nearby Attractions:

- St Ives
- Chysauster Village
- National Trust Trengwainton Garden

https://cornishwalks.com/gpx-files-top-walks-in-west-cornwall/

Elevation Profile

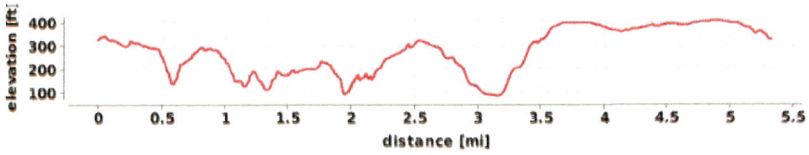

DIRECTIONS:

1. From the car park, head back onto the road and turn left walking towards St Senara's Church. Head past the Tinners Arms, and then turn left, taking the track down to the coast path. At the end of the tarmac lane, walk forwards onto footpath. At the junction with the coast path you want to turn left following the sign to Pendeen. This section of coast path is quite hard going

Mermaid of Zennor

This folktale tells the story of a beautiful and mysterious woman who regularly attended St Senara's Church, Zennor and captured the heart of a local man named Matthew

but the views are glorious, you might even spot the Mermaid of Zennor.

2.   After one and a half miles, you will reach a white cottage sitting just above Treen Cove and near an abandoned set of mining buildings. Cross a small drive and then take the path heading into a hedgerow. This section of the coast path is a bit easier going. At all points stay on the coast path. From the white cottage to the inland turning is a little over a mile. If you wish you can divert out onto Gurnard's Head, enjoy the views and then return to the coast path.

3.   When the coast path comes down almost level with a large beach it's time to turn inland. To access the beach turn right and you will need to climb over boulders. It's a bit of a challenge but it's well worth it at low tide. Otherwise take the footpath left uphill. There is a small stone marker indicating the coast path to Pendeen, but we're going to go left, following the public footpath up to Porthmeor Tin Stamps.

4.   At the top of the hill, explore the tin workings then head towards the top information board and turn left, taking the footpath down into scrubland. As you look ahead you can see the path cutting through a field and on to some cottages. The path cuts through the cottages and heads in a straight direction, until cutting

Trewhella. Unbeknown to the villagers, she was a mermaid who would come ashore to listen to the singing at the church. Eventually Matthew followed her back to the sea, disappearing forever. Inside Zennor Church is a chair covered in mermaid carvings, said to be the very chair she would sit on.

Gurnard's Head

If you walk out onto Gurnard's Head you may see remains of the Iron Age hillfort and accompanying hut circles. Given the stunning cliffs you are also as likely to see rock climbers as well as gannets diving into the sea.

through a small farmyard and up into a field with a standing stone in it.

5.   Exit the field with the standing stone via the stile on the other side of the field and then onto the road. Turn left and walk a quarter of a mile on the road until you get to the Gurnards Head pub. This road is quite busy but it's narrow and full of bends so the traffic is slow. Nonetheless, take care.

6.   When you get to the pub, pass in front of it and take the footpath into the field in front of you via a granite stile. Stick to the left-hand side of the field and exit via a stile via the bottom left corner. In the next field head over to the left-hand side, following the telegraph poles.

7.   Continue along the path until you come out onto a road. Turn left and walk along the road. This is the same road from earlier. Walk for three-quarters of a mile, until the road bends sharply to the right. You need to turn left down an unmade track, there is a yellow post sign saying to coast path. Follow the track towards the cottages, now ignoring any directions to the coast path. Walk past the cottages and when the track bends sharply to the left, walk forwards onto the footpath.

8.   The path now heads in a straight line through several fields, you should be able to see Zennor Church ahead of you. The exits are often marked by white posts, when you finally get to a pair of white posts, walk between these and head between two hedges, past a farm. This is often lined by butterflies and nettles. Highs and lows.

9.   When you come onto the farm track, turn right and head towards the road. At the road, turn left and then take the immediate left-hand lane heading down in Zennor itself and back to the car park.

LINKS:

Penwith History and Landscape
https://www.penwithlandscape.com/

6

MARAZION CIRCULAR – 6 MILES

An excellent walk making a loop of the east and west sections of the **St Michael's Way**. *There are great views at all points, with plenty of facilities along the way. This is a perfect walk to explore the land around St Michael's Mount.*

Length: 6 miles
Effort: Easy
Terrain: Coast path, paved tracks, fields. There are two busy road crossings and an ungated trainline. After the trainline, the path can become waterlogged following prolonged rain or a high tide
Livestock: Some potential for sheep and cattle
Parking: Marazion Station Long Stay Car Park, TR17 0DA
Toilets: Marazion
Café / Pub: Wide range of choices
OS Map: 102

Nearby Attractions:
- Penzance Lido
- Mousehole
- St Michael's Mount

🌐 https://cornishwalks.com/gpx-files-top-walks-in-west-cornwall/

Elevation Profile

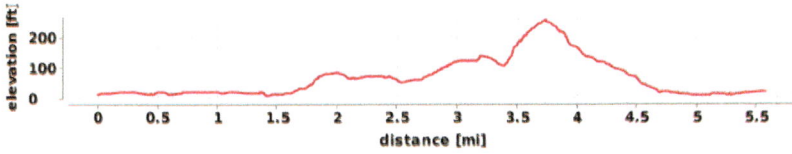

DIRECTIONS:

1. Head to the seafront and then turn right walking through the car parks and along the promenades until you get to the last car park. Carry along the path for just under one and a half miles. This is a shared use path with cyclists so listen out for bells. When you reach the pedestrian flyover, head over the railway line then walk towards the traffic lights and cross the A30. Head up a small residential lane and at the crossroads continue straight ahead following the road signs to Gulval, this section is on the road and can be busy.

2. When you get to the village turn right in front of **Gulval Church** walk past

The Church of St Michael and All Angels, St Michael's Mount

You can explore this church before or after your walk. There has been a church perched high on the island since at least 1135, although it was rebuilt in the fourteenth century.

Access to the chapel and island is ticketed, so check their website for details. The organ used to reside in London, where the insomniac owner

a triangular patch of grass and take the footpath on the left. You need to climb a few steps up through the hedgerow. Follow the footpath through the next few fields as it tracks the road and then at the corner of the last field take the steps on the right back down onto the road. Continue along the road and turn left at the junction, towards Tremenheere Sculpture Gardens.

3.   Just before the entrance to the gardens take the wooden gate to the right-hand side and follow the footpath. Continue past the garden buildings on your left and then take a small wooden footbridge over the stream on your right. The path is clearly laid out through the

would play it at night. At the request of his long-suffering neighbours, he sold it to the fifth Sir John St Aubyn in 1811.

The chapel is one of two pilgrimage locations in Cornwall, the other being St Petroc's Church at Padstow. The island has been in the ownership of the St Aubyns since the sixteen hundreds and still is today.

next set of fields. When the track seems to split by some old buildings, take the upper left-hand fork. Continue along the path as it heads towards the church.

4.   As the path turns into a small lane head uphill. At the T-junction turn left. When you get to **Ludgvan Church** turn right and pass the White Hart pub on your left.

5.   Just after the pub, on the opposite side of the road is a signpost for the **St Michael's Way**. Follow the path down through the fields crossing a small lane as you go. When you reach the next road turn right. There is no footpath and the road can be busy. Follow the road towards a very busy T-junction. Head up onto the

Ludgvan Church

A beautiful church and the resting place of two well-known Cornishmen: William Borlase and Humphry Davy. There is an impressive grave slab for John South (d.1636) as well as a carved figure of a man above the entrance to the church – an early monk, a pilgrim like yourself or even Saint Ludewon. Along with Towednack Church, St. Paul's Church, Ludgvan claims to be the last place to have held mass in Cornish, in the late sixteen hundreds.

Gulval Church

Within the parish boundary lie Ding Dong Mines, the oldest mines in Cornwall and possibly Britain, which have been mined since prehistoric times. The rumour goes that Joseph of Arimathea came here as a trader and brought the young Jesus with him. There isn't a shred of evidence to support this claim, but it is a recent myth.

grass verge and walk over to the traffic island. Cross the road, turn right and then almost immediately take the left-hand stile into a field. Keep to the left of this field and exit at the bottom left.

6.   At the bottom of the trees the path comes out onto a main road that is fast and busy. There is no traffic island. Cross with care and head straight onto the footpath ahead and away from the road. Follow the footpath through the Marazion marshes. At one point you will cross the main London trainline. There are no barriers so take care. The path after the trainline can be very boggy. As you arrive in Marazion leave the footpath via a granite stile and head up on to a small road. Turn left, crossing a stone bridge and then head towards the beach.

7.   From here you can either make your way to St Michael's Mount by boat or causeway, depending on the tide, or you can return to your car.

LINKS:

St Michael's Mount
https://www.stmichaelsmount.co.uk/

Walking with Saints and Tinners by Liz Hurley
https://amzn.to/45qjX8Q

St Michael's Way
This is a newly created path connecting the north and south coasts. It recreates the route that pilgrims and traders would take on their journey from France to Wales and Ireland, when it was safer to walk across Cornwall than sail around Land's End. Instructions for the full route as well as the Saints Way connecting Padstow and Fowey, are in *Walking with Saints and Tinners*, my walking guide covering these longer distance trails. Link left.

7

THE TOWANS AND THE HAYLE ESTUARY – 5 + 2 MILES

A figure-of-eight walk, so if you get tired you can just do a shorter section. The path is nearly all flat, heading up through the sand dunes and along the beach. It then cuts back along the estuary, offering a great opportunity for bird spotting and huge open skies.

Additional Information

Dogs: There is a dog ban on the beach during the summer months. Keep your dog on a short lead and don't leave the coast path.

Tides: Parts of this walk are affected by high tide.

Length: 7 miles
Effort: Easy / Moderate
Terrain: Coast path, sand, footpath, tarmac
Livestock: None
Parking: Any long stay car park in Hayle
Toilets: Hayle
Café/Pub: Cove Cafe, Riviere Towans, Hayle, various
OS Map: 102

Nearby Attractions:
- Paradise Park Wildlife Sanctuary
- St Ives

https://cornishwalks.com/gpx-files-top-walks-in-west-cornwall/

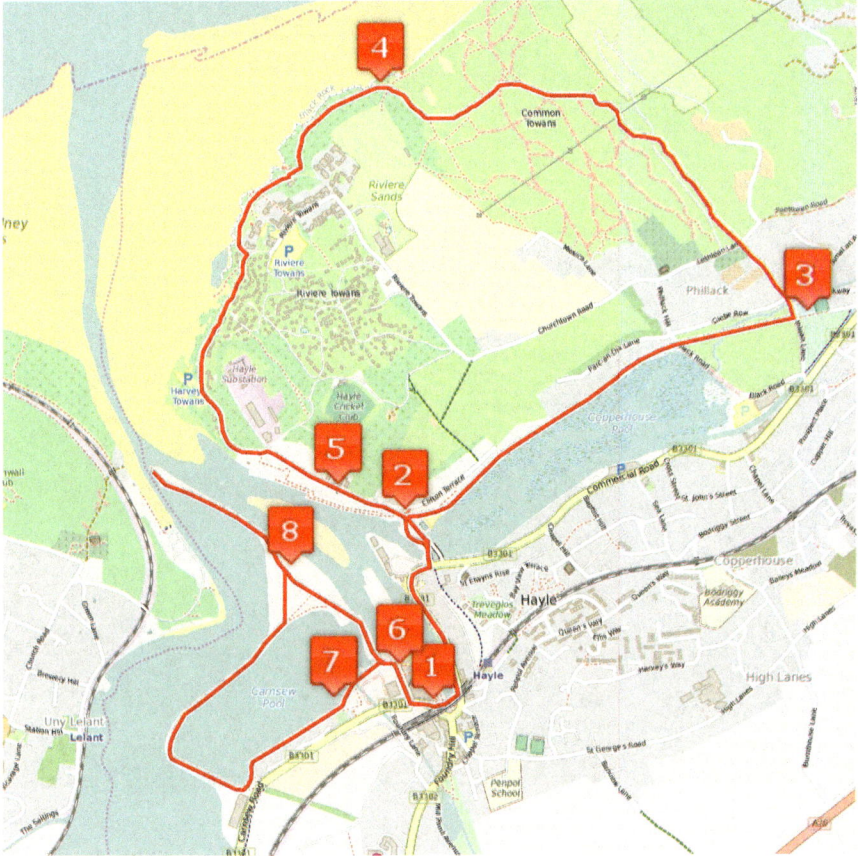

Elevation Profile

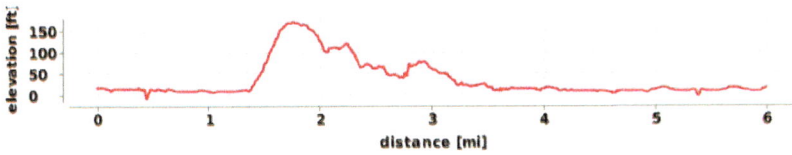

DIRECTIONS:

1.   Start from the front of the Asda superstore and walk towards the viaduct. As you reach the viaduct, turn left and follow the pavement. Do not cross the road or pass under the viaduct. Follow the pavement along Penpol Terrace until it turns to grass. Shortly after the traffic lights on your left, there is a memorial to **Rick Rescorla**. You can continue along the grass heading towards a pasty shop. As you pass the pasty shop, there is a small section where

Rick Rescorla – 9/11
Born in Hayle, Rick joined the army and eventually settled in America, although he regularly came home. On 11 September 2001, Rick, who was supposed to be on holiday, stayed in his office in the South Tower of the World Trade Center to allow a colleague to take time off. Witnessing the events of

you need to walk along the road, if this doesn't appeal cross over to the pavement on the other side and promptly cross back, a few metres later. Now turn left crossing over Jubilee Bridge via the cycle path, following the signs to North Quay.

2.   Once over the river, cross the road, Hayle outdoor swimming pool will be on your right-hand side. Turn right and walk down King George V Memorial Walk. To your right is Copperhouse Pool and to your left is a footpath that takes you through a semi-tropical garden. At the end of King George V Memorial Walk, go through the wooden kissing gate in front of you, onto a footpath that continues alongside Copperhouse Pool.

9/11 unfold from his office, he defied the instructions to stay put and took charge of the evacuation. Using a megaphone, he guided and reassured the Morgan Stanley workers, singing Cornish and Welsh songs to boost morale. Even after everyone had evacuated, Rick chose to go back up the tower to help more people. He was last seen on the tenth floor before the tower collapsed, and his body was never found. His heroic actions saved the lives of thousands of workers and this memorial is a testament to his bravery.

3. The footpath ends at a road. Turn left and walk uphill. When the road turns sharp left at the sign for Lethlean Towans, there is a foot-path sign and a small fight of steps in the wall. Take these and head up into the sand dunes. Follow the obvious path and keep walking forwards. These dunes are a very large system – just keep following the footpath. There is a yellow marker post and the path crosses a private road and heads through a kissing gate in the SSSI (Site of Special Scientific Interest) dunes. Dogs need to be on a lead in this section.

4. This section will depend on the tides. At high tide stick to the coast path, as the beach gets cut off in several sections. Only walk along the beach if you know it is low tide, otherwise you will end up back-tracking. Follow the coast path until you get to a large car park.

5. Stick to the coast path and follow it along North Quay road. Keep the river on your right. You will eventually cross back over Jubilee Bridge. Retrace your footsteps to Asda.

6. You have now walked 5 miles. The next section is an easy 2 miles. From the front of Asda walk along the main road heading right, and then turn right at the traffic lights passing down the side of

Asda. At the end of the building, cross the road and head down a small private road. Turn left just before the bridge.

7.　You are now on a circular path around Carnsew Pool. Turn left and follow the footpath all the way around the water. Some sections of the path are eroded and you will need to mind your step.

Note: At the top of a high tide, a short section of this walk is underwater.

This is the **RSPB Hayle Estuary Reserve** and the whole section is an incredible area for bird spotting. It can also be quite exposed, especially as you walk along the Hayle Estuary nature reserve section.

8.　Three-quarters of the way around, the path opens up and you can turn left and walk out onto the spit. Then head back and continue the rest of the loop around Carnsew Pool until you get back to the bridge, not taken earlier. Cross the bridge and head back towards Asda, where the walk ends.

RSPB Hayle Estuary Reserve

'In cold winters, as many as 18,000 birds have been seen here, because this most south-westerly estuary in the UK never freezes. During spring and autumn it is an ideal place to see migrant wading birds, gulls and terns. In summer, if you are lucky, you may catch sight of an osprey. The reserve is good for walking, with pushchair-friendly paths.' – RSPB

LINKS:

Bird watching
https://www.rspb.org.uk/reserves-and-events/reserves-a-z/hayle-estuary/

A history of Hayle
https://www.harveysfoundrytrust.org.uk/history-heritage/history-of-hayle/

Tide timetable
https://www.tideschart.com/United-Kingdom/England/Cornwall/

THE TOWANS AND THE HAYLE ESTUARY – 5 + 2 MILES

8
....

GODREVY POINT – 2.5 MILES

A lovely short walk that punches well above its weight with a lighthouse, dramatic waves, loads of birds and lots and lots of lovely seals. Don't forget your binoculars!

Additional Information:

Seals: They are around all year but numbers increase dramatically in winter. Sightings can't be guaranteed but January is the best time to see large numbers. Arrive during a low tide when they are all bathing on the sands.

Dogs: Gwithian Sands has seasonal dog restrictions. Dogs are allowed on the coast path all year round but the cliffs mean that dogs need to be on leads for their own safety.

Length: 2.5 miles
Effort: Easy
Terrain: Coast path, paved tracks, sand
Livestock: No farm animals but plenty of seals. You won't get close to them though
Parking: Godrevy National Trust Car Park, TR27 5ED
Toilets: Godrevy National Trust Car Park
Café / Pub: The Rockpool, Godrevy; Godrevy Beach Café
OS Map: 102

Nearby Attractions:
- Paradise Park wildlife sanctuary
- Gweek Seal Sanctuary (18 miles away but relevant)

🌐 https://cornishwalks.com/gpx-files-
top-walks-in-west-cornwall/

Elevation Profile

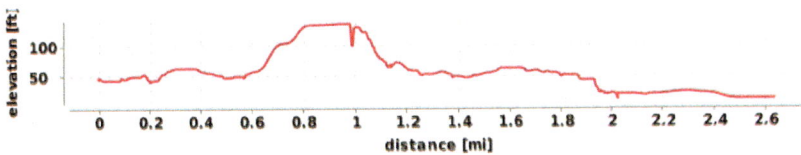

DIRECTIONS:

1. From the first car park, follow the road or path right, keeping the sea on your left. Head along to the second car park on the right-hand side of the road. Continue along the road and past the public loos. Shortly after the loos, take the footpath on the right and head uphill towards a gap in the wooden fence.

2. The path heads up towards the coast path. You are standing on the edge of *very high cliffs* with only a low wooden barrier. Keep behind it, keep hold of small children and ensure all dogs are on leads. Looking down you should hopefully see

Seals and wildlife
The colony of seals at Mutton Cove are grey seals, the larger of our two native seals. Seal numbers in the UK have been steadily rising over the past decade. Even if you don't spot any on the sands below, look out to sea where you may spot them bobbing about. Also keep an eye out for basking sharks and dolphins. Basking sharks are

lots of **seals** resting on the sands below; this is Mutton Cove.

3.　　Now turn left and walk along the coast path with the sea on your right. Ahead of you is **Godrevy Lighthouse**. Continue along the coast path. As you pass the lighthouse, the town you can see across the bay on the far right is St Ives. As you walk back to the car park you will pass some steps down onto the beach. It's a lovely beach but you will need to return to the coast path to continue the

completely harmless, which is just as well as they are the second largest fish in the world, averaging a length of eight metres. Dolphins are year-round residents and love to play in the water – the old Cornish name for a dolphin is *grampus*. Occasionally they will catch a wave with the surfers or simply race alongside the boats.

route. It can be too difficult to return to the car park via the beach.

4.   From the car park, head towards the pay and display meter by the dunes. There are two pay and display machines; when facing the sea you want the one on the left. Take the path by the machine and walk down the steps towards a river. This is the **Red River**.

5.   Facing the river turn left and walk along until you reach the foot bridge. Cross over and turn left, after a few metres turn right into **St Gothian Sands Nature Reserve**. Head directly into the reserve and explore the paths around the lakes until you come back to this point and retrace your steps to the car park.

i Godrevy Lighthouse

The lighthouse stands on Stones Reef, where ships regularly foundered on the rocks and there were decades of calls for a lighthouse there. Following the loss of 40 lives when the *SS Nile* sank in 1854, funds were raised and the light was built in 1858. It was manned by two men who took shifts living on the island, but these days it is automated. It is also the light that inspired *To the Lighthouse* by Virginia Woolfe. To get a closer look at the lighthouse you can take a boat trip from St Ives, although they don't land on the island.

i Red River

The chimney stack that you pass ahead is part of the remains of the Gwithian Stream Works, which removed alluvial tin from the Red River. The high iron deposits in the river stained the water a rusty red colour, giving it its name. Redruth is also named for the red iron deposits: *ruth* is the Cornish word for red.

i St Gothian Nature Reserve

A small wetland area behind the sand dune, St Gothian's is a fabulous place to spot wildfowl. In winter there are lots of passing visitors, including the pretty teal ducks in winter and sand martins in summer.

LINKS:

Godrevy National Trust
https://www.nationaltrust.org.uk/godrevy

9

CARN BREA – 5 MILES

A belter of a walk! Starting at South Wheal Francis Mine, explore the many cathedral-like mining buildings then head across fields and up onto Carn Brea, passing a castle and the Basset Monument that you can see from the A30. Then return on the cycle path passing more mining structures before returning to your car.

Length: 5 miles
Effort: Moderate
Terrain: Small lanes, bridleways, rocky paths
Livestock: Some potential for sheep, cattle and horses
Parking: South Wheal Francis Car Park, TR16 6JX
Toilets: None on route, unless visiting The Countryman Inn
Café / Pub: The Countryman Inn
OS Map: 104

Nearby Attractions:
- King Edward Mine Museum
- Gwennap Pit

https://cornishwalks.com/gpx-files-top-walks-in-west-cornwall/

Elevation Profile

DIRECTIONS:

1. From the car park, make your way to the mining complex. This is the South Wheal Francis Mine sitting on top of the **Great Flat Lode**. Explore the building and then follow the footpath until all the buildings are behind you and you are looking at a grassy field. Take the footpath heading right, towards the houses. Over to the right, on the horizon is a large granite column. This is the Basset Monument that we will be passing on this walk.

The Great Flat Lode
This is a huge lode of tin running for over two miles, lying 30% horizontally. As most lodes run at 70% this was much easier to access. Many of the mining complexes on this route all worked this one lode and it was responsible for a massive boom in the already flourishing Cornish mining industry.

2.   When the path reaches the road turn left. This can be a busy road so take care and join the pavement as soon as you are able. At the right-hand turning, cross the road, and then immediately take the footpath to the right over a set of granite stiles. This runs alongside a pub called The Countryman Inn. The footpath takes you into fields. Stick to the left-hand side and exit via a pair of wooden stiles. In the next field, walk directly across the field, heading in the direction of the telegraph pole, with the sea on the horizon. Pass the pole and head towards a clump of trees. Exit via a stile.

3.   Climb down the stone steps turn left and walk down the track for a few metres, and then turn right, taking a small footpath downhill off of the main track. Enter a field via a wooden stile. Head diagonally down across the field keeping the cottages to your left. In the field on your right there is a curious tree growing out of a stone tump. Exit the field via the far-right corner.

4.   On the footpath, turn right walking uphill. Take the first turning right, and start climbing uphill onto **Carn Brea**. The path is rocky and uneven. At the top follow the path towards the **Basset Monument** and then on to the castle. Having explored the outside of the castle, continue along the path, heading downhill in the direction of two engine houses over on the horizon.

Carn Brea

Carn Brea is a huge outcrop of rock standing 738 feet above sea level and has always been a significant feature on the Cornish landscape. It's said the giant, Bolster, would stand with one foot on Carn Brea and the other over on St Agnes Beacon, ten miles away.

More recently it was owned by the Basset family, who had lived at Tehidy for the past 700 years and were the pre-eminent mining family in the area. They built the castle as a hunting lodge and folly. When the philanthropist Francis Basset died in 1836 the **Basset Monument** was built to honour him. It's an astonishing 90-foot-high hexagonal granite obelisk. It can be seen from miles around and the views from the top look over both coastlines.

5. When the path joins a larger path, turn right, you are now on the cycle trail. At a crossroads, take the left-hand turning, heading downhill on an unmade road. At the bottom of this lane you come to a main road now turn left. Walk for about a quarter of a mile. Just before the 20 mile an hour sign, we rejoin the footpath as it switches back uphill off the right of the road. There is a sign for the Great Flat Lode public bridleway. We're going to be on this for the whole way back to the car park so keep an eye out for bikes and horses. Also see how many chimneys you can count.

6. When the section of the bridleway meets a road, crossover and head up Copper Lane. At the bend in the road, take the right-hand turning continuing along the bridleway. As you pass a large collection of industrial ruins the path splits. Take the upper path following the electricity pylons. At one point, you cross a small lane. At the next split take the right-hand path and follow it through the tunnel. When the path joins a small road, the entrance to your car park is just to the left.

LINKS:

Mining Industry

https://www.cornishmining.org.uk/areas/camborne-redruth-with-portreath

10

GWENNAP PIT AND CARN MARTH – 2.5 MILES

A short walk packed with unusual sights and great views. Gwennap Pit is a deep circular pit used for large gatherings and is a striking feature. Walking on from there you climb up to impressive views, a hidden well and a large quarry lake, perfect for a refreshing swim.

Length: 2.5 miles
Effort: Easy / Moderate. Uneven footpath in places
Terrain: Road and footpath
Livestock: None
Parking: TR16 5HH
Toilets: None. Visitor Centre has seasonal hours
Café / Pub: None on route
OS Map: 104

Nearby Attractions:

- Carn Brea, site of Carn Brea Castle and Basset Monument

https://cornishwalks.com/gpx-files-top-walks-in-west-cornwall/

Elevation Profile

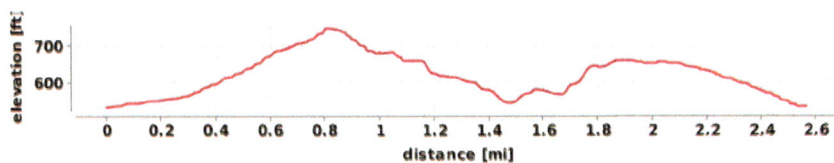

DIRECTIONS:

This walk begins at the front of the Gwennap Pit visitor centre. You can explore the pit at the beginning or the end of the walk.

1. With the visitor centre behind you, turn right and walk along the road for a quarter of a mile, until you reach a right-hand turning marked bridleway and start heading uphill. Ignore all left and rights. As you reach the top, you pass a derelict barn on your left. Now turn right and start heading uphill again until you reach Carn Marth Pool. This is an abandoned quarry

Gwennap Pit
This impressive depression in the ground was possibly created by mining activities. It became a popular location for religious gatherings, and John Wesley preached there on 18 occasions from 1762 to 1789. It was remodelled in memory of Wesley into today's terraced 'amphitheatre' in 1806.

and a popular spot for swimmers and fishermen.

2.   Take the left-hand pass keeping the water to your right. The view to your left looks over west Cornwall towards Falmouth and the Lizard. There is a view-point display that tells you all the distant sights. Halfway down the path on your right-hand side is a red metal gate. Head though the kissing gate and explore the Carn Marth open-air amphitheatre, then return to the path and continue downhill.

Shortly after you leave the amphitheatre keep your eyes peeled for a set of steps to your left leading down to Figgy Dowdy's Well. Having had a quick explore return to the path and head downhill.

Carn Marth Pool

Carn Marth is a small hill once used as a granite quarry. The site is now a registered charity and features a large lake and an open-air amphitheatre, as well as being a place of natural beauty and stunning views.

Figgy Dowdy's Well

This was the source of water for locals and was owned by a woman: 'Figgy Dowdy had a well, on the top of Carn Marth hill, She kept it locked by night and day, Lest people should take her water away.' She went by many names – Figgy Dowdy, Margery Daw and Maggy Figgy – but there is little evidence for her existence, and some of those names might be connected to early Cornish saints associated with fertility. The well was also a site for dolls to be christened on Good Friday, a practice that also takes place at the better known Venton Bebibell, translated as the *well of the little people*.

3.   When you get to the large mining chimney (Pennance Consols) turn right onto the tarmac road. When the road veers left, walk forward onto an unmade road. On the horizon is the Basset Monument, and Carn Brea castle. As the lane ends at a farmhouse, take the small footpath to the left-hand side and continue downhill. Just before the trail joins a road take a sharp right and head up an unmade lane, walking uphill.

4.   As the track crosses another track, take the right-hand turning passing a telegraph pole on the right and a residential garage on your left. You are now on the small track heading uphill. At the junction of a small lane, turn right and continue uphill, passing a South West Water facility.

5.   At the T-junction with the road, turn left. Then, at the next junction turn right. This lane now takes you all the way back to Gwennap Pit. When you reach a small lay-by on you right with parking for four or five cars you are at the pit. Head through the small gate and then cross the pit back to the visitor centre.

LINKS:

Gwennap Pit – A History
https://cornishbirdblog.com/gwennap-pit-the-richest-square-mile-on-earth/

11

STITHIANS RESERVOIR – 5 MILES

An easy walk with no hills and simple directions. Various neolithic features can be explored during low water levels, and there's also an impressive path across the dam.

Length: 5 miles
Effort: Easy
Terrain: Footpath, fields, road
Livestock: None
Parking: Stithians Lake Activities Centre, TR16 6NW (Satnav can be odd for this one but the centre is just by the Golden Lion Inn)
Toilets: Stithians Lake Activities Centre
Café / Pub: Stithians Lake Activities Centre
OS Map: 104

Nearby Attractions:
- Kennall Vale Gunpowder Mill
- Carn Brea

https://cornishwalks.com/gpx-files-top-walks-in-west-cornwall/

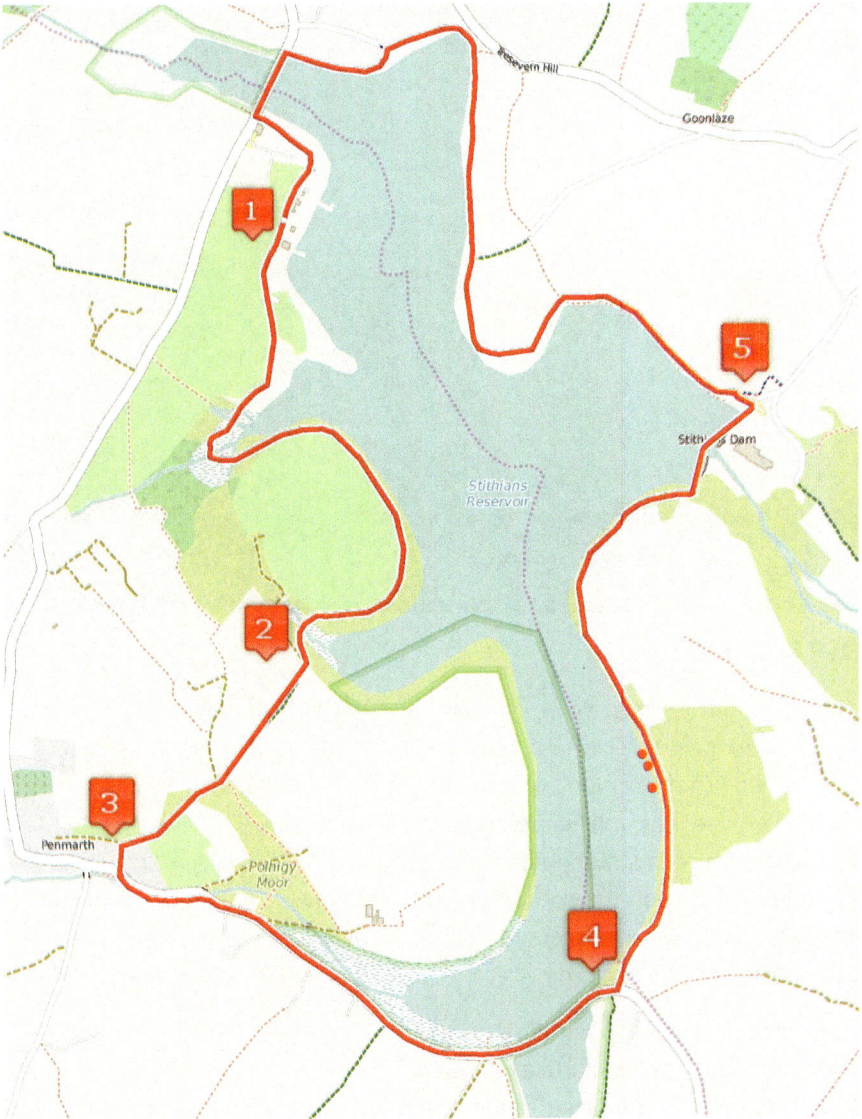

Elevation Profile

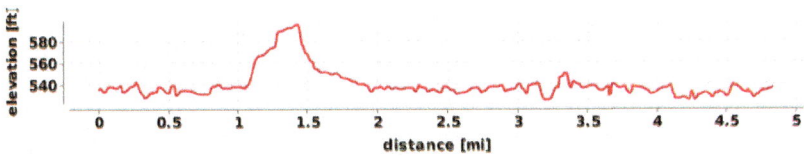

DIRECTIONS:

1. From the main car park, walk past the café on your left. With the reservoir to your left, walk down the path in the direction of Penmarth. There is a signpost labelled 1.5 miles. Quite soon the path seems to fork, take the right-hand fork onto a grass path away from the reservoir.

2. Head through the metal gate, following the signs for Penmarth and onto a small lane. Walk forwards until you reach the hamlet of Penmarth. At the junction with a larger road turn left in the direction of Mossops. Cross the road and take the small footpath that runs alongside.

3. Soon the footpath rejoins the road.

Cup Stones
These are a collection of neolithic marked granite stones. They contain a collection of cup-like depressions and no one knows why they were created. See if you can find them and try and solve the mystery.

There is a verge running along the road if you would prefer not to walk on the road. Continue until you get to the head of the reservoir. Walk past the metal crash bars and then cross over the water. When the road bends right, cross over and now take the footpath on the left.

4.   Follow the path for a mile towards the dam. Depending on the height of the water you may be able to walk along the reservoir bed and examine the **Cup Stones**. There is no indication where they are but it's fun to have a look for them and they are unmistakable when you find them. I have indicated on the map using three red dots where to look for them. This is a very loose guide.

5.   At the top of the reservoir climb the steps and walk along the wall of the dam. At the other end, climb down into a car park and head left towards a green metal bunker. Now take the footpath with the reservoir on your left. When the path comes out onto the road, turn left and walk back towards the activity centre. Turn left just before the Golden Lion Inn and return to your car.

LINKS:

Stithians Lake
https://www.swlakestrust.org.uk/pages/site/activities/category/stithians-lake

Cup Stones
https://acornishjourney.uk/2021/09/08/the-cup-marked-stones-of-stithians/

12

GODOLPHIN ESTATE AND TREGONNING HILL – 6 MILES

A lovely walk that eats up the miles through woodlands and small lanes before heading up to the glorious views from Tregonning Hill and then over to Godolphin Hill, before returning to Godolphin House.

Length: 6 miles
Effort: Moderate
Terrain: Small lanes and footpaths, often uneven paths
Livestock: Some potential for sheep, wild cattle and ponies
Parking: Godolphin National Trust, TR27 6AS
Toilets: Godolphin National Trust
Café / Pub: Godolphin House (entrance fee or free for NT members)
OS Map: 103

Nearby Attractions:
- Goonhilly Earth Station
- Flambards Theme Park

🌐 https://cornishwalks.com/gpx-files-top-walks-in-west-cornwall/

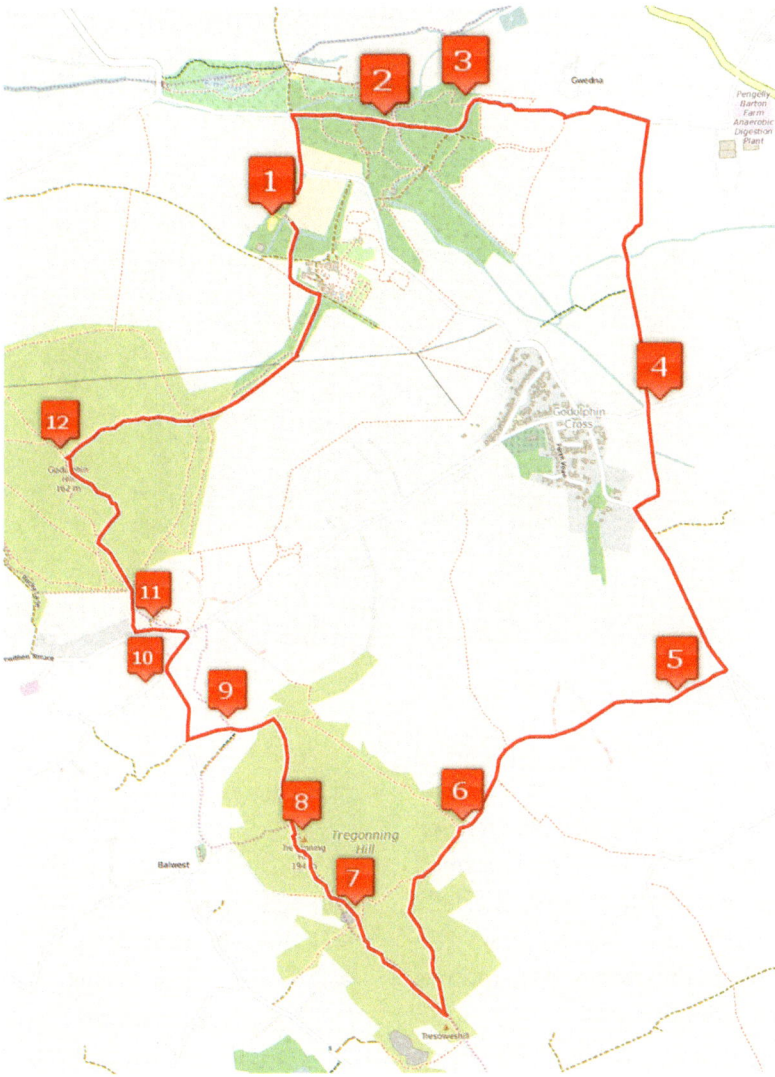

Elevation Profile

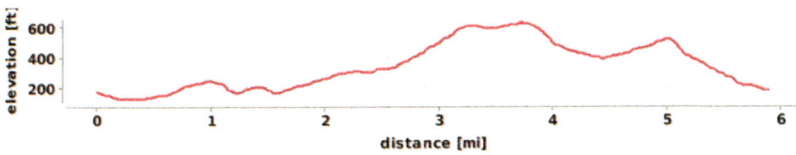

DIRECTIONS:

1. From the car park head back to the main road and walk forwards along the road until you reach a sharp, left-hand bend and small car park. Take the right-hand footpath, via a granite stile heading into the woods. Stay on this path walking towards Godolphin Count House.

2. Pass the Count House on your right and stay on this main path crossing a small stream and continue through the woodland. As the track meets a T-junction, turn left and then take the green permissive footpath sign. It's a little green arrow on a small wooden post.

Godolphin House and Estate
The Godolphin Estate in Cornwall embodies 700 years of rich history, tracing back to the influential Godolphin family. Visitors can explore its 16th-century gardens, a rare unchanged European example from that era, and the periodically open Godolphin House. The grounds also offer a deep dive into Cornwall's significant mining history.

3.   As you reach a kissing gate, head through it into the field and walk uphill, keeping the hedge to your left. Exit at the top-left via a large granite stile and follow the footpath along the fence towards the houses, when you reach a small lane turn right. At the T-junction turn right, following the signpost to Godolphin. Stay on this lane until the next T-junction. Both lanes are small and quiet. At this T-junction cross the road and take the public footpath directly in front of you.

4.   Keeping the stream to your right walk along the meadow and follow the path into the scrubland. Sections of this path can become very boggy. At the gate, climb the stile and head up the drive until it joins the road. At the road turn left, walking uphill. This road is busier and has no pavements, but it's wide with good

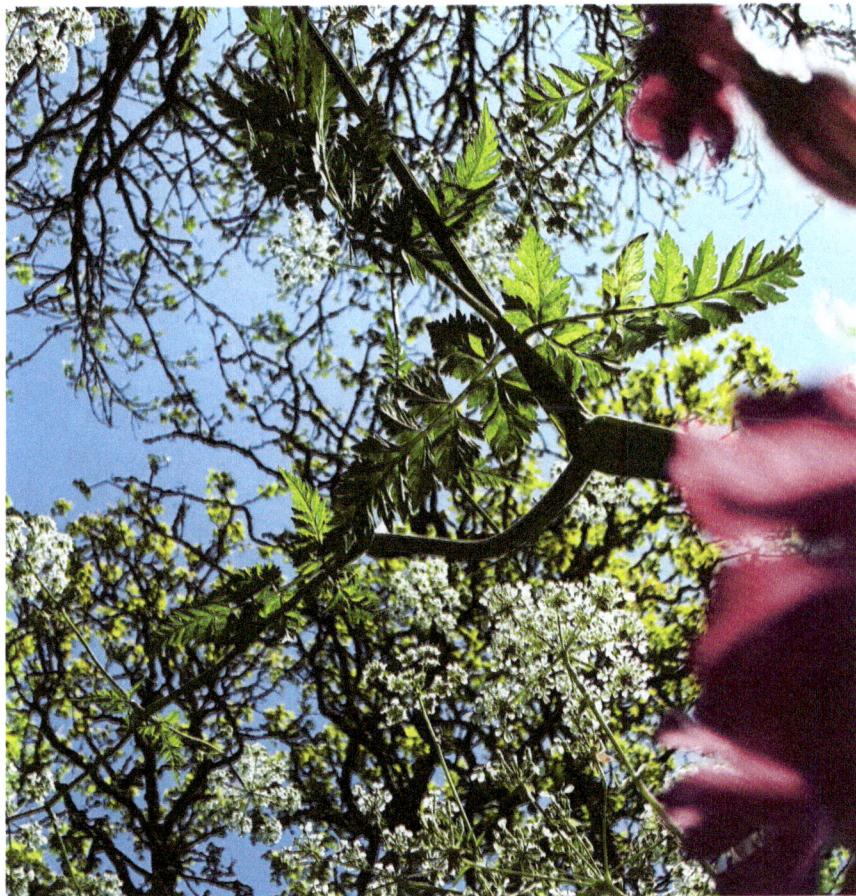

visibility. Take the first right-hand junction to Breage and then immediately turn right again down a small dead-end lane.

5.   As you walk along this lane, you can see the Tregonning Hill in front of you and you should be able to spot on the ridgeline a large granite cross, which is where you are heading. This lane eventually turns into a track. Continue heading uphill, ignoring any left or right turnings.

6.   At the five-bar gate head through and continue uphill. During high summer the bracken can overwhelm the path. When the path forks, take the slightly larger left-hand path. Shortly after the pass begins to level out, you come to a very clear junction with another path. Turn right and walk forwards, with the large stone cross on the horizon ahead of you.

7.   Just as the track becomes hard paved with small stones, there is a plaque to William Cookworthy. Walk a few steps on and you can see a pathway into the ferns on your left, down into the preaching pit. Having explored the pit, come back up to the path and continue uphill. Just as the path begins to head downhill, take the right-hand fork off the stone track and continue towards the granite cross.

8.   When you reach the cross, stop and enjoy the views. Over by the trig point there is a toposcope showing all the distant sights. Now turn right and take

William Cookworthy
Cookworthy was an 18th-century English Quaker and chemist who pioneered the discovery and commercial production of English porcelain. He identified kaolin clay deposits on Tregonning Hill in Cornwall, which were crucial for hard-paste porcelain manufacture. This discovery transformed the English ceramics industry, reducing reliance on imported materials and fostering local production, thus causing the rise of Cornwall as a global player on the china clay stage.

The Preaching Pit
The exact origins of the pit are somewhat shrouded in local lore and history. While it is known that the pit was used for open-air Methodist sermons and gatherings, specific records detailing who exactly carved or constructed the pit are sparse. Some sources attribute the pit to local Methodists of the eighteenth century, who

the footpath all the way down the hill. When you get to an obvious junction in the path, take the left-hand fork and continue downhill, heading in the direction of a large mining chimney.

9.   As you come down to the level of houses and hedgerows you'll pass a metal gate on your right. Continue along the path for a few feet, then with a second metal gate on your left, take the right-hand grassy path, heading downhill away from the farmhouse. Now turn left along a private drive.

10.   When you reach the road, turn right. Stay on the road, ignore the left turn to Boscrege, then take the left-hand turning to Trescowe and Millpool. Head along Ball

were inspired by the visits and teachings of John Wesley and sought a dedicated space for their larger gatherings.

Lane, with the Great Work Mine on your right, pass the turning for the car park and then at the next right-hand turning, head up the unmade road just before a row of houses. As you reach a metal gate take the footpath to the right and head into the trees.

11.   Head over the granite steps and onto Godolphin Hill. From this point, there are four obvious paths. Starting from the left take the third path heading directly uphill, following the small pink footpath posts.

12.   Having reached the summit of Godolphin Hill, turn right and head downhill towards the trees in the valley. There is also a little pink marker leading the way. Keep heading downhill until you reach the wooden gate and kissing gate. Head through and follow the signs back to the Godolphin House and Estate. As you reach the ticket office either explore Godolphin, or turn left and follow the signs back to the car park.

LINKS:

The Godolphin Estate
https://www.nationaltrust.org.uk/visit/cornwall/godolphin

13

LOE BAR – 7 MILES

A glorious walk around Cornwall's largest body of fresh water, then crossing the beach at Loe Bar. This is a walk of two halves. The west side of the lake is a mostly flat, wide, well-laid path. It is popular with families, dog walkers, scooters and cyclists, as well as other walkers. The east side is a different beast; the path is often unmade and hilly, running through trees and fields. I love this path as it's so quiet, but it is also more challenging. The views are worth the effort though.

Additional Information:

Swimming: There is no opportunity to swim anywhere here. The lake can suffer from blue algae and the beach has a dangerous undertow which has resulted in several drownings.

Flooding: In winter or after heavy rain the eastern half may be impassable due to flooding. In this case, simply walk the west side to the sea and back.

Length: 7 miles
Effort: Easy / Moderate
Terrain: Hardcore, sand, grass, earth
Livestock: None
Parking: Fairground Car Park, Helston, TR13 8WN
Toilets: The Stables, part of the National Trust Penrose Estate
Café / Pub: The Stables
OS Map: Explorer 103

Nearby Attractions:
- Flambards Theme Park
- Cornish Seal Sanctuary
- The Lizard, Britain's most southerly point

Elevation Profile

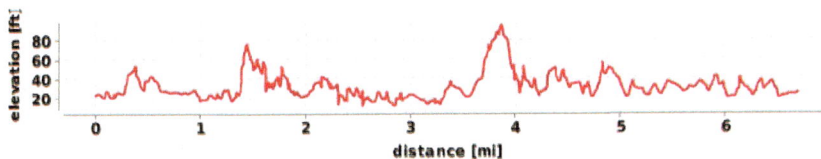

DIRECTIONS:

1. Make your way to the concrete road behind the car park and turn right. The car park is on your right and the waterworks on your left as you walk away from town. After half a mile as the road veers sharp left, turn right onto the bridleway.

The route is signposted along the way with yellow arrows on the posts indicating the footpath. As ever, follow the yellow arrows whenever you see them.

The Loe

The Loe was once the estuary of the River Cober but with the emergence of the shingle bar the estuary became a lake. This can cause flooding issues in the nearby town of Helston, as the river has no means of rapid dispersal

In summer they may be hidden in the undergrowth. Most of the path is shared with the bridle/cycle way, and these are the blue arrows. If the lower footpath is flooded you can always follow the blue cycle path, on the higher path.

2.   The path opens onto pastureland, which can be wet and muddy. Stick to the left and follow the trail through the field and into the trees. As the trail opens into a triangular clearing, take the lower path. There are two main paths in these woods one for walkers and one for bikes. The footpath is always the lower of the two. Follow the path, keeping the Loe on your right and head upwards until you reach a gate.

in heavy rains. In the past the Loe Bar would be cut, allowing a channel for the lake to empty onto the beach and down to the sea. New pumps have now been installed on the beach, removing water from the lake to mitigate the need for another cut.

3.   Head through a gate and into a large field. Ahead of you, you should be able to see the sea for the first time. Pass through a second gate and then turn right along a small lane. Take the path to the right of the cottage and then continue walking alongside **the Loe**.

4.   Take the right-hand turning across the wooden causeway and turn right at the end. Take the lower right-hand path. As you get closer to the sea, the trail is increasingly sandy until the point when it becomes pure sand.

5.   As you come onto the beach you need to turn right and head towards the

Penrose Estate

The second half of this walk travels through the more formal part of the Penrose Estate. Penrose is a National Trust estate, and while the house itself is privately owned the rest is available to explore. There is an interesting little bathhouse as well as pretty walled gardens. These kitchen gardens are attached to the stables, which now act as a great house up on the cliff edge. This beach is known as the Loe Bar. **You CANNOT swim here.** Head off the beach and up to the house. Take the trail in front of the house and follow the lower route signposted 'Stables via Loe Pool'.

6.   You are now on the return journey and the route is wide, flat and well made. This side of the **Penrose Estate** is clearly signposted and easy to navigate. For these reasons, this section of the walk can be busy with a wide range of users. At The Stables there are loos and a good café, plus a walled garden.

7.   From The Stables, take the bridge across the valley, turn right at the T-junction and walk back to your car park. To visit the small bath house, turn left at the T-junction; you can see it in the fields on the right of the path. Having explored turn round and head home.

café. The house itself was the centre of a recent fascinating family history story, as it was inherited by an unknown son whose claim was established through a DNA test.

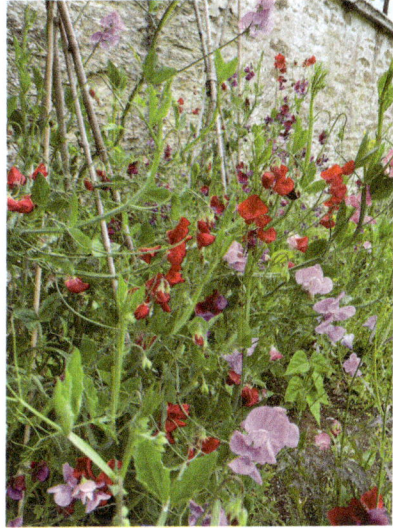

LINKS:

The Penrose Estate
https://www.nationaltrust.org.uk/visit/cornwall/penrose

14

FRENCHMAN'S CREEK – 3 MILES

An atmospheric walk through woodlands and along the shores of the creek, discovering a hidden chapel and romantic smuggling haunts. The path is easy to follow and the walk is short although some of the hills are a little puffy. At the end of the walk take a dip in the sea or enjoy a feast at any of the dining options.

Additional Information:
Optional Walk: This walk can be linked with the Helford to St Anthony Walk.

Length: 3 miles
Effort: Easy / Moderate
Terrain: Paved tracks, fields, a few small lanes
Livestock: None
Parking: Either Helford or Helford Passage across the creek. You'll need to book a ferry across, but parking in Helford Passage can save a long drive if coming from the north or east
Toilets: Helford
Café / Pub: The Shipwright Arms; Holy Mackerel Café; The Ferry Boat Inn (across the water)
OS Map: 103

Nearby Attractions:
- Glendurgan and Trebah Gardens (north of the river)
- Goonhilly Earth Station (south of the river)

https://cornishwalks.com/gpx-files-top-walks-in-west-cornwall/

Elevation Profile

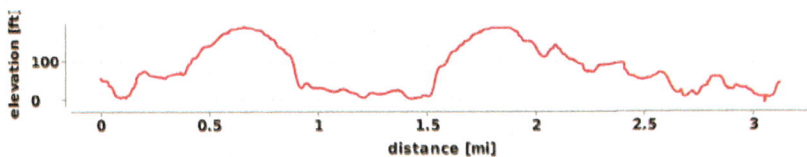

DIRECTIONS:

From the ferry: Head off the boat and make your way along the footpath and into the village, passing the Shipwright Arms on you left. When you get to the bridge cross the creek and turn left up the lane.

From Helford car park: Walk back to the road and turn right heading into the village. Pass the wooden bridge, keeping the creek to your right and continue up the lane.

1.   As the lane turns into a public footpath follow the signs towards Kestle Barton. When the footpath comes to a right-hand turning, cross the stream and continue along the path to Kestle Barton. Follow the path up through the trees and alongside a field. Leave via the gate and then walk through a collection of farm buildings until you come to a small lane.

2.   Walk across the road and take the footpath directly ahead then continue with the field on your left, following the path into the trees. When you come to a fork take the right-hand path and continue downhill through the trees. Now walk along **Frenchman's Creek**.

Towards the end of the creek the path splits; take the left-hand creek-side option.

3.   Follow the path until it turns uphill and joins a private lane. Turn right, away from the creek, and head uphill along the lane. At the top of the hill take the right-hand turning and follow the road uphill, following signs to Penarvon Cove. At the first left turn take the small lane downhill, signposted to Helford via Penarvon Cove.

4.   Halfway down the lane take the left-hand turning heading back uphill. Follow this lane past Tall Trees house at the T-junction turn left and leave the lane. You are now taking the footpath into Pengwedhen Woods. This is a small, looped path that begins and ends at this point. Take the left-hand path and follow it all the way around until you get to **St Francis's Chapel** halfway along the lower

Frenchman's Creek
This secluded and enchanting inlet, flanked by lush greenery and cascading cliffs, offers a serene and idyllic setting. Its tranquil waters and hidden coves evoke a sense of mystery and adventure befitting the romantic escapades depicted in Daphne du Maurier's *Frenchman's Creek*, a historical novel set in 17th-century Cornwall. It follows the daring adventures of Lady Dona St Columb, who rebels against her stifling aristocratic life by engaging in a passionate romance with a French pirate, finding freedom, love and self-discovery along the Cornish coast.

path. Step off the path to explore the chapel and then continue back to the start of the loop.

5. Back on the lane follow it downhill as you pass through a collection of sheds and boathouses and take the footsteps down to Penarvon Cove. Walk across the head of the beach, take the footpath and head into the trees back towards Helford. As the path pops out onto little concrete drive, turn left and walk downhill.

St Francis's Chapel
This tiny chapel was built almost a hundred years ago in memory of Dr Leo O'Neill, a local man, and is dedicated to St Francis of Assisi, the patron saint of animals. This is a beautiful and simple chapel; there is a striking statue of St Francis within, and the eaves are lined with small offerings.

6. When the road turns right there is an option to turn left towards the ferry. If you came via the ferry turn left now and head back across the water. Otherwise turn right into the village. Pass the Shipwright Arms and cross the creek at the bridge. From here turn left and retrace your steps to the car park.

LINKS:

Helford Ferry
https://helfordriverboats.co.uk/the-ferry/

***Frenchman's Creek* by Daphne du Maurier**
https://amzn.to/3ZrVOfN

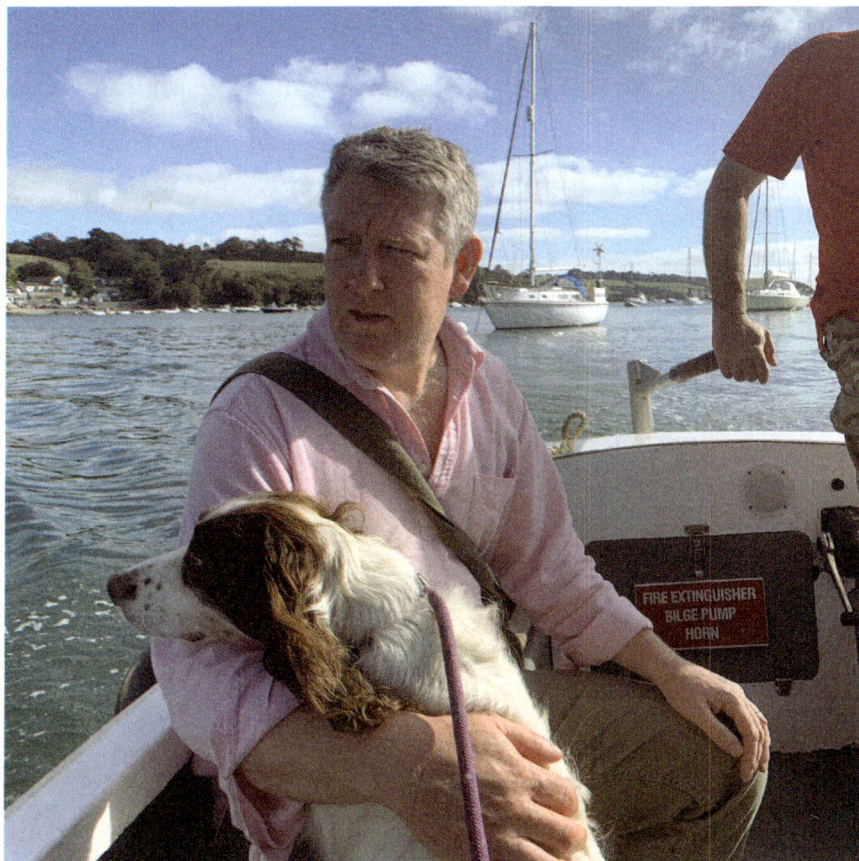

15

HELFORD TO ST ANTHONY – 5 MILES

An easy walk with great creek and sea views, pretty villages plus a chance to swim and take a river ferry. All rounded off with a choice of fabulous places to eat.

Additional Information:
Optional Walk: This walk can be linked with the Frenchman's Creek Walk.

Length: 5 miles
Effort: Easy
Terrain: Coast path, paved tracks, fields, a few small roads
Livestock: Some potential for cattle
Parking: Either Helford, or Helford Passage across the creek. You'll need to book a ferry across, but parking in Helford Passage can save a long drive if coming from the north or east
Toilets: Helford
Café / Pub: The Shipwrights Arms; Holy Mackerel Café; The Ferry Boat Inn (across the water)
OS Map: 103

Nearby Attractions:
- Glendurgan and Trebah Gardens (north of the river)
- Goonhilly Earth Station (south of the river)

https://cornishwalks.com/gpx-files-top-walks-in-west-cornwall/

Elevation Profile

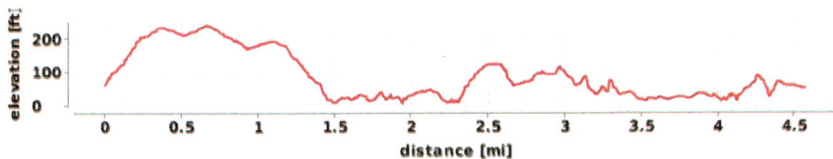

DIRECTIONS:

1. This walk starts at the Helford car park. Walk out to the road and then turn left and walk uphill. Just before the road veers left take the footpath on the right-hand side and head up into a field. The fingerpost says Manaccan. Halfway up the second field, head left along a private drive.

2. When you rejoin the road, turn right and follow the road all the way into the village of **Manaccan**, crossing one small

Trigging
Cockling, it seems, is a Good Friday tradition that's been around since forever, and it is widely practised around this stretch of water. Some versions claim it was because a tight-fisted landowner grudgingly allowed

road, then head into the village and make your way downhill to the church. Passing the church on your left, follow a small lane until you reach Vicarage Lane on your right, it is directly opposite one of the entrances to the churchyard. The lane is also a public bridleway, stay on it until the path splits, then take the right-hand fork towards St Anthony.

3. As you come into a small hamlet, turn left and follow a grassy path downhill

foraging only once a year. Another tale ties it to the Catholic practice of fish-only Fridays. Either way, Good Friday cockling is now as much a tradition as overcooking the turkey at Christmas. The action of rake-wielding foragers, by the way, is known as *trigging*.

as the lane becomes a footpath again. The path follows a pretty stream but it can get quite wet underfoot. Head through the gate at the bottom and turn left onto a small road. This is a public highway so although it's quiet, watch out for cars.

4.   Just as the road begins to climb take the footpath to the right signed Gillan Creek. This is a beautiful path winding through the trees with the creek to your right. When it rejoins the road turn right and walk into the village of St Anthony. You can swim here if the tide is in or wait until you reach the beaches on the other side of the headland. This is also a popular spot for **trigging**.

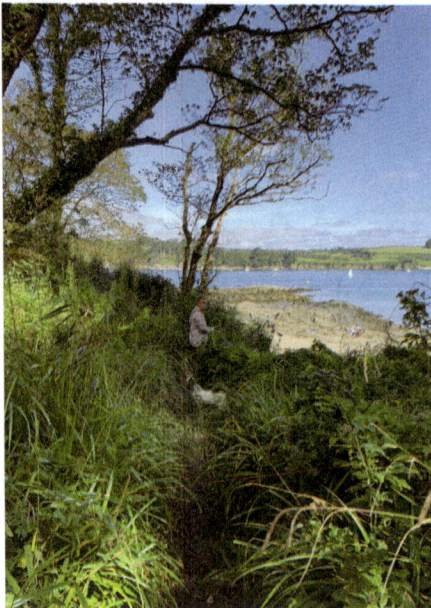

Manaccan

Captain Bligh was once wrongfully arrested as a spy and held in the Manaccan Vicarage outhouse. He was interviewed by the local Justice, who deemed it to be a case of mistaken identity and they then shared a meal of woodcock and wine together. Law and order ran differently back then.

The fig tree growing out of the church is said to be 300 years old and cursed. So don't pick the leaves!

5.   Stay on the road passing the church on your left. Just after the church there is a footpath to your right. You are now on the coast path. Head uphill, through a gate and onto a field. At the kissing gate you can turn right up to the headland for stunning views across Falmouth Bay. Otherwise, turn left and walk along the coast path back to Helford.

6.   There are two beaches along the way that are easily accessible, the second is larger and sandier. As you get closer to Helford the coast path follows the road; follow the signposts until you are back in the village. Make sure you spot the turning off the road just before Helford River Sailing Club. Take a few steps up on the left to continue on the coast path as it circumnavigates the club and leads into the car park.

LINKS:

Helford Creek
https://cornishwalks.
com/a-good-friday-ramble-out-on-
the-helford-creek-discovered-an-
annual-tradition/

Helford Ferry
https://helfordriverboats.co.uk/
the-ferry/

16
·······

MULLION – 3.5 MILES

A pretty walk across the Lizard heathland with glorious views out to sea and over Mullion Island. A big climb at the beginning and then mostly flat before the descent back into the picturesque fishing cove. Mullion Island is a wildlife reserve so don't forget your binoculars.

Length: 3.5 miles
Effort: Easy / Moderate
Terrain: Coast path, paved tracks, fields. Almost road free. Lots of granite stiles
Livestock: Some potential for cattle or ponies
Parking: Mullion Cove Car Park, TR12 7EX
Toilets: Mullion Cove
Café / Pub: Porthmellin Tea Rooms, on the harbour (seasonal)
OS Map: 103

Nearby Attractions:
- Kynance Cove
- The Lizard Peninsula
- Flambards Theme Park

🌐 https://cornishwalks.com/gpx-files-top-walks-in-west-cornwall/

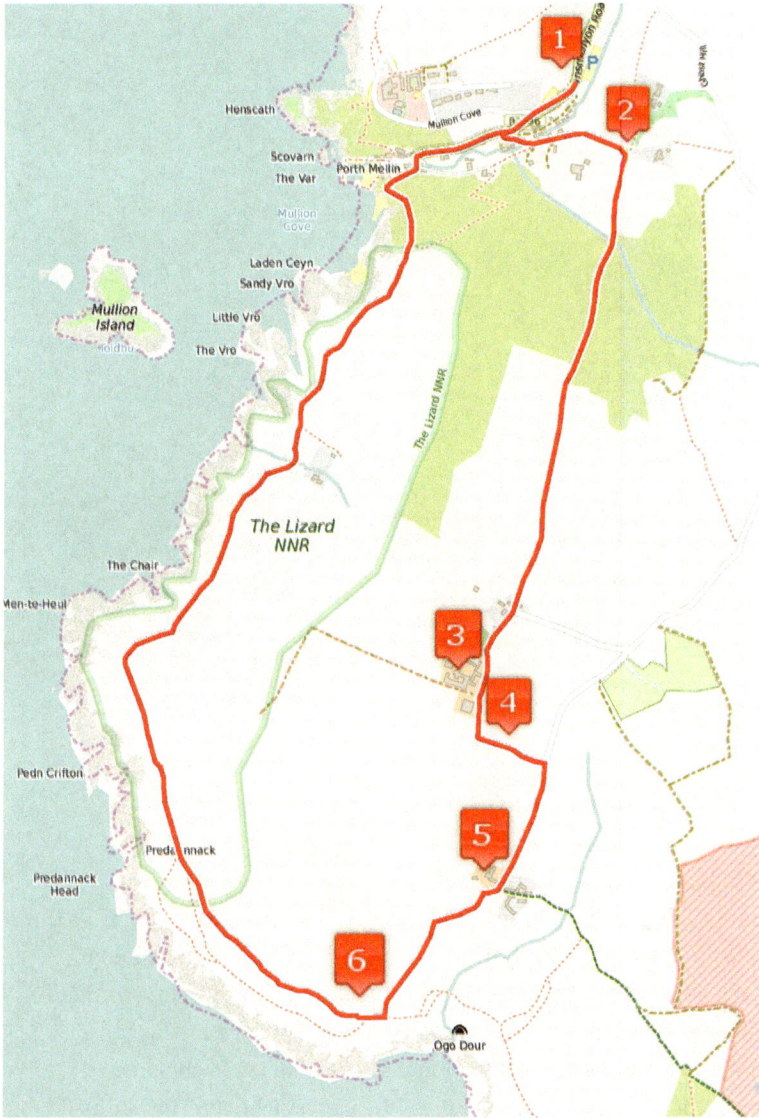

Elevation Profile

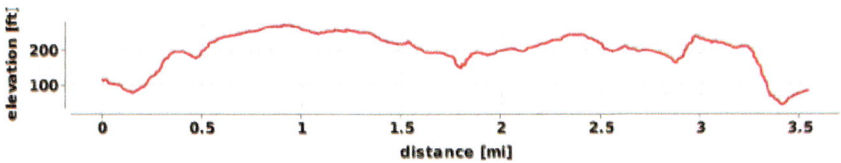

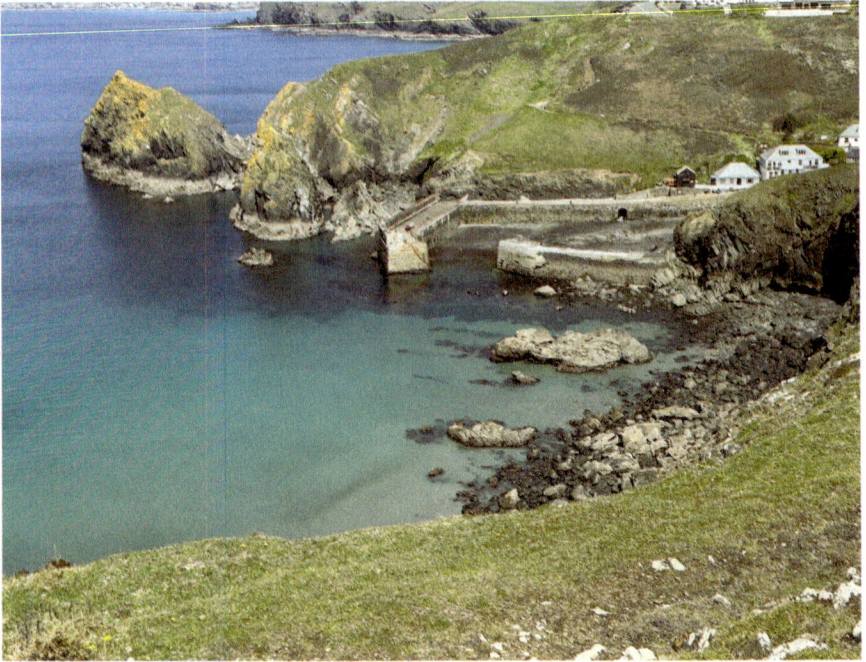

DIRECTIONS:

1. From the car park head onto the road and walk downhill. You are going to be walking directly on the road for a few hundred yards. Take the first left off the road and then walk along a track passing Mullion Cove Park on your left, and head uphill. After quite a slog uphill, you'll see a granite standing stone on your right, in front of a hedge. Just before the stone, to the right, are two metal gates and the path continues between them.

2. The path now follows the left-hand side of a field. As you leave the field,

Lizard National Nature Reserve

The Lizard Peninsula in Cornwall is a hotspot for biodiversity, boasting a unique blend of flora and fauna due to its mild climate and varied habitats. This walk takes in various highlights of these habitats including its heathlands, where you can find rare plants like the Cornish

the path continues between two gorse hedges and crosses a few small streams before climbing uphill again. This section is all part of the Lizard National Nature Reserve. Cross a huge stone stile and into a large field and head through the next three fields, sticking to the left-hand hedge. In the third field there is a stone cross. Be sure to look behind you at this point as you can start to see the sea. Head towards the cottages, the exit is directly alongside a house, over a series of granite stiles. Walk forwards onto a road and continue in the same direction.

heath and various species of orchids. The coastline provides a habitat for a variety of seabirds, including cormorants and shags, as well as marine life like grey seals and dolphins. Inland, the mixed woodland and scrubland areas offer sanctuary to a variety of animals, including badgers, foxes and numerous species of butterflies and birds.

3. Just before Predannack Manor farm take the footpath to your left. You are now on a wide path passing a granite building on your right. The footpath

now turns into a small grassy track. Keep the agricultural barns to your right.

4.   Cross over a granite stile and into a field. The path now goes directly across the field. Look in the direction of the telegraph pole opposite and you can see the exit in the hedgerow. There may be cattle in this field. Climb into the next field and keep the hedge to your immediate left. In the corner of the field, take the wooden stile out to a small lane. Turn right and head downhill until you reach a small National Trust car park.

5.   Head to the top right-hand corner of the car park and climb the granite steps and take the footpath over to your right following the signpost: 'Mullion Cove via Coast Path 2 miles'. At the end of the footpath take the wooden stile into a field, following the yellow permissive path sign. The views from hereon in are pretty spectacular. Head towards the small outcrop of rocks, and from them, walk down to a wooden stile in the fence below.

6.   You are now on the coast path, turn right and head back to Mullion Cove. There are several sheer drops along this section so don't get too close to the edge and keep dogs on a lead. As you approach the cove the descent is quite steep. Once in the village head onto the road and walk up back to the car park.

LINKS:

Mullion Harbour
https://www.nationaltrust.org.uk/visit/cornwall/mullion-cove

17

COVERACK – 7.5 MILES

A belter of a walk! Dappled, shady groves, tumbling streams, small fields and glorious sea views on the return journey. There's a wonderful café along the way and a great beach to swim at, plus a pretty village. After prolonged rain the first section of the walk can be very boggy.

Length: 7.5 miles
Effort: Moderate / Challenging. Stout footwear is strongly recommended
Terrain: Coast path, tracks, fields, lanes
Livestock: Some potential for sheep
Parking: Coverack Car Park, TR12 6TF
Toilets: Coverack; St Keverne; Porthoustock
Café / Pub: Roskilly's, St Keverne
OS Map: 103

Nearby Attractions:
- Goonhilly Earth Station
- The Lizard Peninsula
- Kynance Cove

https://cornishwalks.com/gpx-files-top-walks-in-west-cornwall/

Elevation Profile

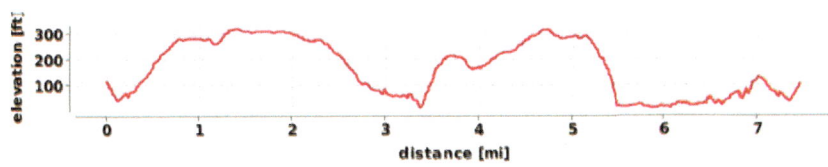

DIRECTIONS:

1. From the car park, walk down to the seafront and then turn left onto the coast path. This section is on a small residential lane and climbs out of the village. Just after the last house there is a footpath sign pointing to St Keverne. Take this path, climbing over a wooden stile.

2. The path climbs quickly through trees. It is strewn with boulders and there is a small stream running through it. This can be very muddy but incredibly pretty. The path continues through small fields and sections of woodland. It is clearly laid out, crossing kissing gates and stiles. When you get to the top of a large field, pass through a wooden kissing gate and you should see a yellow fingerpost sign. Then

Giant's Quoits
Before their collapse in early 1966, the Giant's Quoits, a striking formation of natural granite rocks, were originally situated on the cliffs of Manacle Point. Following their fall they were repositioned in 1967 near Rosenithon to accommodate the expanding operations of the St Keverne Stone Company quarries.

Porthoustock
Porthoustock is primarily known as a quarrying village, associated

at the fork take the left-hand path and continue on a slight incline up. Shortly after the second kissing gate turn right, following the fingerpost. When the track comes out onto a concrete lane, turn right.

3.   Follow the lane into a series of farm buildings, walk to the end and then take the footpath heading away from the farm. It is clearly signposted. The path opens onto a small road: head up the hill to-wards a thatched cottage. When the road comes to an end, walk forwards towards the fingerpost. The path now splits and you need to take the left-hand path. The path through the fields is well-trodden and easy to follow. Leave the final field via a gate.

4.   The path now continues by crossing the road and taking the footpath opposite. However, Roskilly's is just a hundred yards to your right and you might like to stop for refreshments. Once you've enjoyed your ice cream come back to this spot. Take the footpath through the fields to St Keverne. When the path joins the road walk forwards and head to the church.

5.   The footpath continues through the churchyard, so climb the stone steps and follow the main path to the left, through the graveyard, ignoring any left- or right-hand turns. Exit via two kissing gates and follow the path downhill. Cross a concrete road and take the footpath opposite,

with the extraction of stone. The stone quarried from this area, including high-quality granite and gabbro, has been used in various construction projects both locally and internationally.

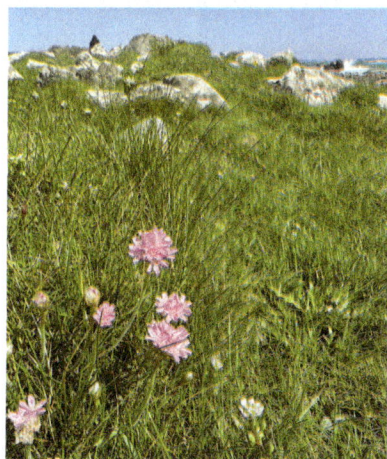

(slightly to your left), go over the next set of coffin stiles and then follow the path down into the trees and follow a small river. The path gradually leaves the river and climbs slightly until you reach a tarmac road. Turn left walking up the road until you pass a pretty house on your left, the footpath is on your right.

6. The path gives way to a small lane of pretty thatched cottages. Walk towards the sea: you are now on the coast path. This section of the path travels along the road. Follow the road down into **Porthoustock**. From the beach if you look out to sea you are looking at the site of the infamous **Manacles**. Return to the road and then head out of the village on the other side from which you came in.

7. This section is really steep. At the first junction turn left and carry on uphill. This road is very quiet. Halfway up the hill on your right-hand side, the coast path cuts off the corner of the road cutting across the field. However, this misses the **Giant's Quoits**. Carry on walking uphill on the road and then turn right, passing the Giant's Quoits.

The Manacles

The Manacles are a set of underwater rocks off the Cornish coast near the Lizard Peninsula, notorious for being treacherous to navigate. The area has claimed over a hundred ships and the lives of those on board over the centuries, earning it a reputation as one of the most hazardous maritime areas in the British Isles.

Recognised for their unique and diverse marine ecosystems, the Manacles were designated a Marine Conservation Zone in 2013. This helps to protect the varied flora and fauna in the area, which includes rare species of corals, sponges and fish. Given the shipwrecks and wildlife this is a very popular site for experienced divers.

8. Follow the road into the hamlet of Rosenithon.* Walk through the hamlet and after a third of a mile, take the left-hand turning to Trythance. This is a very small lane. Towards the end of the lane there are decorative ponds on the left. You can leave the lane and follow the path uphill until the path rejoins the road and a junction. Take the left-hand turn, to Dean Point, half a mile.

*Note. Normally the coast path heads back down to the sea at this point. However, there is currently (2023) a year-long diversion in place, so continue to follow

Steps 8 & 9. However, it may be that by the time you read this the path will be reinstated. In which case, head down to the sea and turn right and jump to Step 10, remembering that there will be an additional mile of shoreline.

9. Head uphill and as the road bends to the right take the footpath across the field directly ahead of you. Exit the field, rejoin the road, and turn left. Follow the lane until it ends at a turning for a quarry with lots of No Entry signs. Take the hardcore track to the right. Follow this track for half a mile, all the way downhill to the coast path. It is very steep in sections but there is a handrail.

10. Once on the coast path turn right. The next mile and a half is flat walking, just above the shoreline. It is a very pretty section of the coast path although sections can be boggy depending on recent rainfall. Eventually the path starts to climb uphill into the treeline until you get to the junction you took at Step 2. Now retrace the last third of a mile back to the car park.

LINKS:

Shipwrecks
https://www.submerged.co.uk/manacles/

CORNISH LANGUAGE

The words you see and hear in Cornwall look very different to those in the rest of England. This is because Cornwall once had its own language, which was in use up until the 1700s and only finally died out in the 1800s. The Cornish language is part of the Celtic family and shares many similarities with Welsh and Breton. In fact, many Welsh speakers recognise a lot of Cornish place names and sayings from their own language.

Today Cornish is being spoken once more, and although there are no native speakers yet the language is all around you. The Cornish dialect has developed through a blend of two languages, English and Cornish, which means that things aren't always pronounced the way you might expect.

This quick little guide should help you through some of the more popular sayings and words, and help with translation of some of the place names.

Dialect

Aw right/alright: 'Hello, how are you?' The response is, 'Aw right, you?'

Backalong: sometime in the past

Brock: badger

Cousin Jack/Jill: This was the name given to Cornish men and women who went to work in the mines overseas. It is also the name given to a certain type of stone wall, where the topping stones stand up like jagged teeth.

Crib: mid-morning snack

Dreckly: 'I'll get around to doing that soon.' It's been likened to the Spanish mañana, but it's not as urgent!

Furze: gorse. The lovely bright yellow spiky bush that blooms all year round in Cornwall.

Geddon: lots of meanings for this one, depending on where you are and the context of the sentence, e.g. 'Are you joking?', 'That's incredible', 'Hello', 'Goodbye'.

Heller: a child throwing a proper tantrum

Lover: friendly greeting 'Alright, lover.' Can be used with a total stranger, male or female

Mizzle: not quite mist or rain but certainly wet

Ope: a small little alleyway

Proper job: this is excellent

Right on: I agree with you

Some: very. It's some hot, some wet, some busy

Teasy: tearful, fretful

Up North, Away, Up Country, Foreigner: basically, all these phrases refer to anyone or anywhere past the River Tamar

Wasson: What's On? What's going on?

Cornish Words

The Cornish language is most visible in the place names. There is a little rhyme that notes how much the language is still in effect in Cornwall.

> *By their names Tre, Pol, Pen, ye shall know the Cornishmen.*

If you look at the list below you can work out what a lot of local towns and villages mean.

Bos/Bod: home or dwelling

Carn: a pile of rocks

Cos: a forest, a wood or group of trees

Eglos: church

Hayle: an estuary

Lan: a sacred enclosure, such as a church or monastery

Maen (Mên): a stone

Pen: an end of something, a headland or head

Perran: named after St Piran / St Perran, the patron saint of tinners

Pol: a pool

Porth (Port): a bay, port or harbour

Ros: a moor, heath or common

Ruth: red

Towan: sand dunes

Tre: a homestead and its nearby buildings, literally a town

Venton/Fenton: a spring or fountain

Wheal: a mine

OTHER WALKING GUIDES IN THE SERIES

To discover more of Cornwall try one of the following walking guides, with more on their way.

CORNISH WALKS SERIES

WALKING IN THE MEVAGISSEY AREA
9780993218033 | https://amzn.to/2FsEVXN

WALKING IN THE FOWEY AREA
9780993218040 | https://amzn.to/2r6bDtL

WALKING WITH DOGS BETWEEN TRURO AND FOWEY
9780993218057 | https://amzn.to/2jd83tm

TOP WALKS IN MID CORNWALL
9780993218064 | https://amzn.to/2LTxUI8

TOP WALKS IN EAST CORNWALL
9780993218088 | https://amzn.to/2XeBNZf

CYCLING IN CORNWALL
9781913628055 | https://amzn.to/3uNwJy9

WALKING WITH SAINTS AND TINNERS
9781913628062 | https://amzn.to/3ELWpj2

For more information visit https://cornishwalks.com/

WITH THANKS

Creating a walking guide is a massive undertaking with many parts and even more people. A book starts with me poring over maps and looking at green dotted lines: I'll establish a walk on paper and then I go and walk it. This stage often reveals issues such as blockages or difficult access, and walks will get dropped at this stage or moved on to a second walk. This is where friends and family come in. I give them the instructions and then walk with them and watch where they find my instructions hard to follow.

Once the instructions are clear they get sent out to test walkers. I am grateful for my lovely volunteers who have walked all across west Cornwall following my instructions – they have been invaluable. They have caught little errors, making the instructions even more robust, and have also contributed ideas and suggestions using their own local knowledge. I would like to thank Jacquie Stembridge, Alison Gunderson, Linda Handyside, Tracey Dell, Clare Baylis, Ali Siddall, Lynda Blackman, Anne Luke and Brindley Hosken. They have all been wonderful and so generous with their time.

After the text is finalised, the manuscript goes off to my editors and designers. Denise Cowle is my text editor and does a wonderful job making my prose clean and precise. Anna Gow is my proofreader for both the text and the artwork layout. Stephanie Anderson of Alt 19 Creative is my typesetter and Sally Mitchell is my cover designer. Each and every one of them is incredible to work with.

As you can see from the book you are holding, everyone involved has contributed to making a beautiful guide. And finally, you are the last piece of the jigsaw puzzle. Thank you for buying this book and I hope you enjoy discovering new routes.

Printed in Great Britain
by Amazon

48967433R00069